Contents

D0771747

Introduction

Who is this book for?

Writing for IELTS will prepare you for the IELTS Academic Writing test whether you are taking the test for the first time, or re-sitting the test. It has been written for learners with band score 5-5.5 who are trying to achieve band score 6 or higher.

The structured approach, comprehensive answer key and model answers have been designed so that you can use the materials to study on your own. However, the book can also be used as a supplementary writing skills course for IELTS preparation classes. The book provides enough material for approximately 50 hours of classroom activity.

Content

Writing for IELTS is divided into 12 units. Each unit focuses on a topic area that you are likely to meet in the IELTS exam. This helps you to build up a bank of vocabulary and ideas related to a variety of the topics.

Units 1–11 cover the key stages of the writing process: everything from analysing the task to proof-reading a completed response. Every exercise is relevant to the test. The aims listed at the start of each unit specify the key skills, techniques and language covered in the unit. You work towards Unit 12, which provides a final practice IELTS Writing test.

Additionally, the book provides examination strategies telling you what to expect and how best to succeed in the test. Exam information is presented in clear, easy-to-read chunks. 'Exam tips' in each unit highlight essential exam techniques and can be rapidly reviewed at a glance.

Unit structure

Each of the first 11 units is divided into 3 parts.

Part 1 introduces vocabulary related to the topic as well as a selection of the most common academic words and expressions needed for the writing functions covered in the unit. A range of exercises gives you the opportunity to use the vocabulary – clearly and effectively – in a variety of contexts. The vocabulary is presented using Collins COBUILD dictionary definitions.

Part 2 provides step-by-step exercises and guidance on the key stages of the writing process. Both writing Task 1 and Task 2 are covered in each unit. There are guided questions and worked examples to show you what an effective IELTS response looks like. Useful expressions and grammatical forms are highlighted, and there are exercises to help you to develop good range and accuracy in your writing. You are encouraged to apply what you have learnt while at the same time writing your own responses to task questions.

Part 3 provides exam practice questions for Task 1 and Task 2 in a format that follows the actual exam. You can use this as a means of assessing your readiness for the actual exam.

Answer key

A comprehensive answer key is provided for all sections of the book including recommended answers and explanations for more open-ended writing tasks. There are model answers for all of the writing questions. For one of the practice exam questions in each unit, two model answers are given – one of them annotated. This shows you that a variety of approaches to each writing task can be taken.

Using the book for self-study

If you are new to IELTS, we recommend that you work systematically through the 12 units in order to benefit from its progressive structure. If you are a more experienced learner, you can use the aims listed at the start of each unit to select the most useful exercises.

Each unit contains between three and four hours of study material. Having access to someone who can provide informed feedback on writing practice exercises is an advantage. However, you can still learn a lot working alone or with a study partner willing to give and receive peer feedback.

Ideally, you should begin each unit by working through the **Part 1** vocabulary exercises. Try to answer the questions without looking at a dictionary in order to develop the skill of inferring the meaning of unfamiliar words from context. This is important because dictionaries cannot be used during the actual exam. Avoid writing the answers to vocabulary exercises directly into the book so that you can try the exercises again once you have completed the unit.

Work through the **Part 2** writing exercises from beginning to end. It is important to study the examples given in order to become familiar with the type of writing required. Doing this will also help you become a perceptive – and critical – reader of your own work. The grammar points covered should be thoroughly mastered so that during the actual exam you can focus on the higher order skills of planning and effectively communicating your response. All learners, including those who are working on their own, should attempt the writing tasks as writing is a skill that can only be improved through extensive practice. At the same time, you should aim to become well-informed about a wide variety of subjects, not just those covered in the book. The IELTS Writing test can cover almost any topic considered to be within the grasp of a well-educated person.

Part 3 contains exam practice with timed questions. This gives you the opportunity to practise writing to a time limit. If you find this difficult at first, you could focus first on writing a high-quality response of the correct length. Then you could start to reduce the time allowed gradually until you are able to write an acceptable answer within the time limit. You should become familiar enough with your own hand writing so that you can accurately estimate the number of words you have written at a glance. Model answers should be studied to identify the underlying approach and effect on the reader. Try not to memorise essays or reports or to attempt to fit a pre-existing response around another exam question. If you work systematically through the book, you should develop the skills and language to effectively express your own responses to unseen exam questions on the day.

The International English Language Testing System (IELTS) Test

IELTS is jointly managed by the British Council, Cambridge ESOL Examinations and IDP Education, Australia.

There are two versions of the test:

- Academic
- General Training

Academic is for students wishing to study at undergraduate or postgraduate levels in an English-medium environment.

General Training is for people who wish to migrate to an English-speaking country.

This book is primarily for students taking the Academic version.

The Test

There are four modules:

Listening	30 minutes, plus 10 minutes for transferring answers to the answer sheet NB: the audio is heard *only once*. Approx. 10 questions per section Section 1: two speakers discuss a social situation Section 2: one speaker talks about a non-academic topic Section 3: up to four speakers discuss an educational project Section 4: one speaker gives a talk of general academic interest
Reading	60 minutes 3 texts, taken from authentic sources, on general, academic topics. They may contain diagrams, charts, etc. 40 questions: may include multiple choice, sentence completion, completing a diagram, graph or chart, choosing headings, yes/no, true/false questions, classification and matching exercises.
Writing	Task 1: 20 minutes: description of a table, chart, graph or diagram (150 words minimum) Task 2: 40 minutes: an essay in response to an argument or problem (250 words minimum)
Speaking	11–14 minutes A three-part face-to-face oral interview with an examiner. The interview is recorded. Part 1: introductions and general questions (4–5 mins) Part 2: individual long turn (3–4 mins) – the candidate is given a task, has one minute to prepare, then talks for 1–2 minutes, with some questions from the examiner. Part 3: two-way discussion (4–5 mins): the examiner asks further questions on the topic from Part 2, and gives the candidate the opportunity to discuss more abstract issues or ideas.
Timetabling	Listening, Reading and Writing must be taken on the same day, and in the order listed above. Speaking can be taken up to 7 days before or after the other modules.
Scoring	Each section is given a band score. The average of the four scores produces the Overall Band Score. You do not pass or fail IELTS; you receive a score.

IELTS and the Common European Framework of Reference

The CEFR shows the level of the learner and is used for many English as a Foreign Language examinations. The table below shows the approximate CEFR level and the equivalent IELTS Overall Band Score:

CEFR description	CEFR code	IELTS Band Score
Proficient user	C2	9
(Advanced)	C1	7–8
Independent user	B2	5–6.5
(Intermediate – Upper Intermediate)	B1	4–5

This table contains the general descriptors for the band scores 1–9:

IELTS Band Scores		
9	Expert user	Has fully operational command of the language: appropriate, accurate and fluent with complete understanding.
8	Very good user	Has fully operational command of the language, with only occasional unsystematic inaccuracies and inappropriacies. Misunderstandings may occur in unfamiliar situations. Handles complex detailed argumentation well.
7	Good user	Has operational command of the language, though with occasional inaccuracies, inappropriacies and misunderstandings in some situations. Generally handles complex language well and understands detailed reasoning.
6	Competent user	Has generally effective command of the language despite some inaccuracies, inappropriacies and misunderstandings. Can use and understand fairly complex language, particularly in familiar situations.
5	Modest user	Has partial command of the language, coping with overall meaning in most situations, though is likely to make many mistakes. Should be able to handle basic communication in own field.
4	Limited user	Basic competence is limited to familiar situations. Has frequent problems in understanding and expression. Is not able to use complex language.
3	Extremely limited user	Conveys and understands only general meaning in very familiar situations. Frequent breakdowns in communication occur.
2	Intermittent user	No real communication is possible except for the most basic information using isolated words or short formulae in familiar situations and to meet immediate needs. Has great difficulty understanding spoken and written English.
1	Non user	Essentially has no ability to use the language beyond possibly a few isolated words.
0	Did not attempt the test	No assessable information provided.

Marking

The Listening and Reading papers have 40 items, each worth one mark if correctly answered. Here are some examples of how marks are translated into band scores:

Listening: 16 out of 40 correct answers: band score 5
23 out of 40 correct answers: band score 6
30 out of 40 correct answers: band score 7

Reading 15 out of 40 correct answers: band score 5
23 out of 40 correct answers: band score 6
30 out of 40 correct answers: band score 7

Writing and Speaking are marked according to performance descriptors.
Writing: examiners award a band score for each of four areas with equal weighting:

- Task achievement (Task 1)
- Task response (Task 2)
- Coherence and cohesion
- Lexical resource and grammatical range and accuracy

Speaking: examiners award a band score for each of four areas with equal weighting:

- Fluency and coherence
- Lexical resource
- Grammatical range
- Accuracy and pronunciation

For full details of how the examination is scored and marked, go to: www.ielts.org

1 Gender roles

Part 1: Vocabulary

1 Many people believe that men and women are different in fundamental ways. Decide which words are commonly associated with men and which words with women.

   a aggressive
   b authoritative
   c competitive
   d compliant
   e gentle
   f strong
   g vulnerable

2 A knowledge of abstract nouns is essential for academic writing. Complete the sentences 1–6 with the noun form (singular or plural) of the adjectives in brackets.

   Example: _Aggression_ is commonly considered a masculine trait. (aggressive)

   1 I believe that men and women have different _____. (strong)

   2 _____ is not an exclusively feminine characteristic. (gentle)

   3 Many men have difficulty showing _____. (vulnerable)

   4 Some people have difficulty working with female _____ figures. (authoritative)

   5 Women are often praised for _____, whereas men are praised for leadership. (compliant)

   6 There is some evidence that girls are better at cooperation, while boys are happier when they are in _____ with one another. (competitive)

3 In IELTS Writing Task 1, you have to summarise information which is usually presented in a visual form. Match the figures 1–6 with the headings a–f. Then complete the descriptions with the words i–ix. The first one has been done for you.

   a bar chart
   b diagram
   c flow chart
   d _line graph_
   e pie chart
   f table

   i   comparisons
   ii   axis
   iii columns
   iv   _trends_
   v   percentage
   vi   vertical
   vii segment
   viii features
   ix   stage

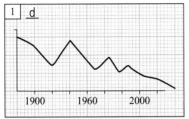

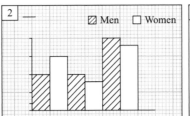

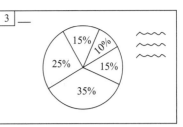

This type of figure can be used to show (7) __iv__. The horizontal (8) _____ often indicates time, and the (9) _____ axis often shows what changes over time.

These figures are useful for illustrating (10) _____ between items or categories of items. This one compares men and women.

You can use a figure like this to show how a whole is composed of parts. Here, each (11) _____ indicates a (12) _____ of the whole.

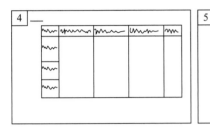

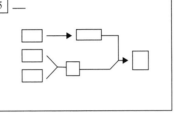

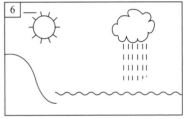

You should present data like this if you need to give precise numbers. This example contains four rows and five (13) _____.

This type of figure is useful for representing a process. Each box represents one (14) _____ in the process.

Figures like this are also used to represent a process. They can also illustrate the (15) _____ of an object.

4 **In IELTS Writing Task 2, you have to write an essay discussing opinions and the reasons for holding these opinions. Complete the Task 2 essay questions 1–5 with the words a–e.**

a agree **b** consider **c** feel **d** see **e** view

1 Many people think that boys and girls learn better when they are educated separately. How do you _____ about this view?

2 In your _____, what should be done to promote equality of opportunity for men and women?

3 Do you _____ boys to be naturally more aggressive than girls?

4 Many people argue that governments should intervene in the labour market to ensure that more women are promoted to positions of power. To what extent do you _____ with this practice?

5 What do you _____ as the main reasons for gender inequality in the workplace?

Part 2: Practice exercises: Task 1

1   Read the Task 1 instructions below and answer the questions 1–4.

WRITING TASK 1

You should spend about 20 minutes on this task.

The chart below shows the numbers of male and female research students studying six science-related subjects at a UK university in 2009.
Summarise the information by selecting and reporting the main features, and make comparisons where relevant.

Write at least 150 words.

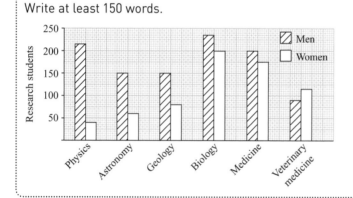

    1   How long should you spend on this task?

    2   How many words do you need to write?

    3   Will you score higher marks if you include all the information in the chart?

    4   Are you expected to give your opinion about the information?

2   Your answer to Task 1 should include a brief introductory paragraph, 1–3 body paragraphs and, if you wish, a brief concluding paragraph. Read the sample answer on page 11 and answer the questions 1–6 below.

    1   What information does the introduction contain?

    2   What is the main focus of the first body paragraph?

    3   What is the main focus of the second body paragraph?

    4   What is the purpose of the first sentence in each of the body paragraphs?

    5   What is the purpose of the second and third sentences in each body paragraph?

    6   What is the purpose of the conclusion?

The bar chart shows the gender distribution of students doing scientific research across a range of disciplines at a UK university in 2009.

In five of the six disciplines, males outnumbered females. Male students made up a particularly large proportion of the student group in subjects related to the study of inanimate objects and materials: physics, astronomy, and geology. The gender gap was particularly large in the field of physics, where there were five times as many male students as female students.

Men and women were more equally represented in subjects related to the study of living things: biology, medicine, and veterinary medicine. In biology, there were nearly as many women (approximately 200) as men (approximately 240). This was also true of medicine. Veterinary medicine was the only discipline in which women outnumbered men (roughly 110 women vs. 90 men).

Overall, the chart shows that at this university, science-related subjects continue to be male-dominated; however, women have a significant presence in fields related to medicine and the life sciences.

3   Study the pie chart and read the sample answer below. Underline and correct the mistakes the writer has made.

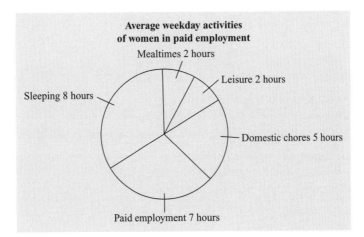

Average weekday activities
of women in paid employment
Mealtimes 2 hours
Leisure 2 hours
Sleeping 8 hours
Domestic chores 5 hours
Paid employment 7 hours

The pie chart shows the numbers of hours devoted to various activities in the average working woman's day. Women spend the largest proportion of their waking day working in paid employment (seven hours) and doing domestic chores (five hours). Women have on average relatively little time for themselves; only two per cent of their day is devoted to leisure activities and two per cent to mealtimes. Overall, the chart shows that working women are busy every day of the week.

> **Exam tip:** Always look carefully at what figures represent. If they represent percentages, you must use expressions such as *a large/small/higher/lower percentage of men* ... If the figures give numbers, you can write *many/more/most/few/fewer men* ...

Part 2: Practice exercises: Task 2

4   Read the Task 2 instructions below and complete the statements 1–4 by circling a or b.

> You should spend about 40 minutes on this task.
>
> Write about the following topic:
>
> In spite of the many advances women have made in education and employment, they continue to be at a disadvantage when it comes to pay and promotion. In your view, what should be done to promote equality of opportunity for men and women in the workplace?
>
> Give reasons for your answer and include any relevant examples from your own knowledge or experience.
>
> Write at least 250 words.

1   You should spend
   a   more time on Task 2 than on Task 1.
   b   the same amount of time on Task 2 and Task 1.

2   In your response you should mainly
   a   explain why women are at a disadvantage.
   b   suggest solutions to the problem of inequality in the workplace.

3   To support your opinion, you should
   a   give reasons and examples.
   b   give reasons or examples.

4   You have to write
   a   more than 250 words.
   b   fewer than 250 words.

5   Read the sample answer on page 13 and the explanatory comments in the boxes. Complete the boxes 1–5 by adding the comments a–e. Then answer questions 1–5.
   a   an example
   b   summary of your main points
   c   a better solution
   d   an acknowledgement that there are difficulties
   e   advantage of this solution

description of the situation and problem	In many parts of the world, there is now greater equality between working men and women. Nevertheless, women still tend to earn less and enjoy fewer promotions than men.
an opposing opinion	Some would argue that this situation will correct itself over time. However, in my view, there is much that can be done to address the problem constructively.

your opinion and plan

one possible but not ideal solution

an advantage of this solution

a disadvantage of this solution

One possible approach would be for governments to force employers to promote the same numbers of men and women and to pay them the same salaries. This would certainly tackle the problem quickly. However, measures like this would probably be seen as excessive and difficult to enforce.

1 _____

an advantage of this solution

A more feasible approach would be for governments themselves to take the lead by ensuring that their male and female employees earn the same for equivalent work and that women are promoted fairly. This would help to establish gender equality as a norm and set a good example for companies in the private sector. Countries, such as Sweden and Iceland, which have done this are often regarded by others as socially-advanced models.

2 _____

another solution

3 _____

To further encourage equality, companies could be required to publish figures on the rank and average earnings of men and women in their workforce. Evidence of large inequalities would create a bad impression. In order to avoid bad publicity, companies might consider it worthwhile to pay fairer wages and promote more women to management positions.

4 _____

restatement of your opinion

5 _____

It is true that the problem of gender inequality in the workplace will probably not be solved quickly. However, that is not a reason to avoid taking action. Governments can encourage change by showing the way forward and taking advantage of the need for companies to present themselves as fair and reasonable.

1 How long is the introduction?
2 How many body paragraphs are there?
3 How many main points are there?
4 In what order are solutions discussed: from strongest to weakest or from weakest to strongest?
5 What is the main purpose of the conclusion?

6   Read the essay questions 1–5 below and indicate the type of essay (a–d) you need to write. (See the Exam information box above.) Underline the words in the essay question that helped you decide.

1   Why do you think women generally hold fewer positions of power?

2   In many parts of the world, unemployment among men is rising whilst the number of positions in jobs traditionally held by women is increasing. Do you think that women will overtake men as the main wage earners?

3   To what extent should governments intervene in the labour market to ensure that men and women are paid the same amount for equivalent work?

4   Although there has been a large increase in the numbers of women who go out to work, women continue to do a disproportionate amount of housework and childcare. What can be done to promote greater equality between men and women within the home?

5   Some people believe that boys and girls behave differently only because society teaches them that they are different. What is your view?

Part 3: Exam practice

WRITING TASK 1

You should spend about 20 minutes on this task.

> *The chart shows the percentage of male and female teachers in six different types of educational setting in the UK in 2010.*
>
> *Summarise the information by selecting and reporting the main features, and make comparisons where relevant.*

Write at least 150 words.

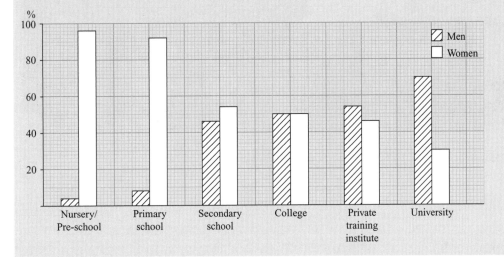

WRITING TASK 2

You should spend about 40 minutes on this task.

Write about the following topic:

> *Women and men are commonly seen as having different strengths and weaknesses. Is it right to exclude males or females from certain professions because of their gender?*

Give reasons for your answer and include any relevant examples from your own knowledge or experience.

Write at least 250 words.

2 Diet & nutrition

Aims: Describing a line graph | Using tense and time expressions | Taking a position
Generating ideas for an essay | Presenting arguments and reasons for your opinion

Part 1: Vocabulary

1 Match the expressions 1–9 with the correct definitions a–i.

1	organic food	a	physical weakness resulting from lack of food or poor diet
2	dietary supplement	b	fruit and vegetables available at particular times of the year
3	obesity	c	food that needs little preparation and can be used at any time
4	fast food	d	a diet without meat or fish
5	genetically modified food	e	food containing genes which have been altered
6	seasonal produce	f	condition of being very overweight
7	convenience food	g	tablets or foods taken to improve nutrition
8	malnutrition	h	food grown without artificial fertilizers or pesticides
9	vegetarianism	i	food that can be obtained quickly from a restaurant

2 The verbs a–h can all be used to describe line graphs. Match each expression with the part of the graph it best describes.

a   rise (rose, risen)
b   fall (fell, fallen)
c   peak (-ed, -ed)
d   reach (-ed, -ed) its lowest point
e   level (-led, -led) off
f   dip (-ped, -ped)
g   remain (-ed, -ed) the same
h   fluctuate (-d, -d)

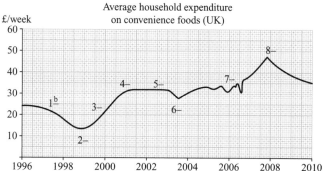

Average household expenditure on convenience foods (UK)

3   *There be* + noun (+ *in*) can also be used to describe trends.

Example: *There was a rise in fast food consumption.*

Write the noun form of the verbs 1–7.

Example: *rose   rise*

1 increased
2 peaked
3 decreased
4 dipped

5 fell
6 dropped
7 fluctuated

4   The adjectives a–g can be used to describe the degree of change represented in a line graph. Adjectives are placed before the noun.

Example: *There was a sharp rise in fast food consumption.*

Match each adjective with the line that it best describes.

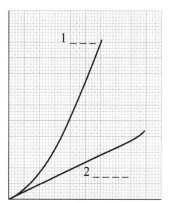

a gradual
b moderate
c modest
d sharp
e dramatic
f slight
g steep

5   Adverbs can also be used to describe the degree of change. Adverbs come after the verb.

Example: *Fast food consumption rose sharply.*

The sentences 1–5 on the left describe trends using *there be* + adjective + noun. Complete the sentences on the right using the corresponding verb + adverb.

Example: *There was a steep increase in sales of convenience food.*	*Sales of convenience food increased steeply.*
1 There was a dramatic decrease in the use of dietary supplements.	The use of dietary supplements _____.
2 There was a modest dip in levels of obesity.	Levels of obesity _____.
3 There was a slight fall in the production of genetically modified food.	The production of genetically modified food _____.
4 There was a significant drop in levels of malnutrition.	Levels of malnutrition _____.
5 There was moderate fluctuation in the availability of seasonal produce.	The availability of seasonal produce _____.

Part 2:   Practice exercises: Task 1

1   In order to describe a line graph, you need to understand the time frame and use the correct tense. Study the graph below. Then read the passage and draw a solid line (___) under examples of the past tense, a dotted line (......) under examples of the present perfect tense, and circle the expressions which refer to the future. Then answer questions 1–4.

Consumption of fresh fruit and vegetables rose steadily from 1970 to 1990, and then levelled off. There was a dip in the early and mid 1990s, and then a further rise until it reached a peak of 500g per person in 2005. Since then consumption has fluctuated. Over the next ten years, consumption is expected to fall steadily. Between 2020 and 2030, it is also projected to decline, but more gradually.

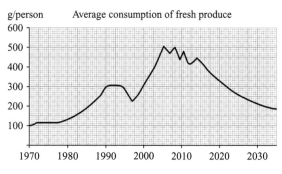

1   When should you use the past tense in describing a line graph?

2   When should you use the present perfect tense?

3   What other expressions can you use for future trends?

4   When would you use the present tense?

2   Complete the passage below using verbs, adverbs, adjectives and nouns. Make sure you use the correct verb tenses. The first one has been done for you.

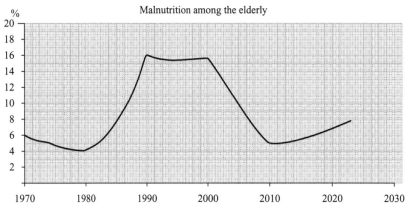

The percentage of malnourished elderly people in the EU <u>fell gradually</u> between 1970 and 1978. Over the following seven years, it (1) _____ (2) _____, until 1990, when it (3) _____ at 16 per cent. After falling slightly, the rate of malnutrition (4) _____ for a decade. Since 2000, there (5) _____ a (6) _____ fall. Over the next ten years, it is (7) _____ to (8) _____ (9) _____.

3   When describing a line graph, you should also indicate precisely the time you are referring to. Use the expressions a–e to complete the passage below.

%   Use of dietary supplements by children

a   over the next .../for the following ...
b   thereafter
c   from ... to/between ... and
d   until
e   in (x2)

The percentage of children using supplements is at its highest level (1) _____ January _____ March. It then falls sharply and fluctuates (2) _____ two months. Supplement use continues to fall gradually (3) _____ it reaches its lowest point (4) _____ August. (5) _____, it increases gradually during the autumn months and more sharply (7) _____ December.

> **Exam tip:** You can also use *from ... to* to describe the amount of change.
> Example: *The percentage of children taking dietary supplements fell from 21 per cent in January to 6 per cent in March.*
> Notice that the start and end points are indicated by *in (in January ... in March)*. If you find this word order confusing, put the time frame at the start of the sentence and the amount of change at the end.
> Example: *Between January and March, the percentage of children taking dietary supplements fell from 21 per cent to 8 per cent.*

4   Compare the two descriptions of a graph on obese adults. Underline any differences that you find.

Description 1
The percentage of obese adults rose steadily from 8 per cent in 1950 to 15 per cent in 1970. There was a slight dip, and then there was a gradual rise until 1990. It rose steeply for the next ten years, and then it levelled off. It has risen even more sharply, and it is projected to peak at 35 per cent in 2010 and then it will level off.

Description 2
The percentage of obese adults rose steadily from 8 per cent in 1950 to 15 per cent in 1970. There was a slight dip, followed by a gradual rise until 1990. After rising steeply for the next ten years, it levelled off. Since then, it has risen even more sharply. It is projected to peak at 35 per cent in 2010, and level off thereafter.

Now use the expressions: *followed by ...*, *after + -ing* and *since then* to rewrite the description below. Remove any unnecessary words.

Between 1996 and 1999, expenditure on convenience foods fell gradually from approximately £25 per week to half that amount. It rose sharply over the next three years and then levelled off at £30 per week. It remained the same for over two years. It dipped briefly and then rose slightly. Between 2005 and 2007 it fluctuated. It rose sharply and peaked at nearly £50 per week in 2008 and then started to fall.

Part 2:   Practice exercises: Task 2

5   Once you have analysed the title, you need to generate ideas. It helps to begin by identifying how you feel about the topic. Look at the statements 1–5 below and mark them according to how closely they represent your opinion. SA (Strongly agree), A (agree), D (disagree), SD (strongly disagree)

1   We should return to more natural methods of food production, such as organic farming, even if this means that we produce food less efficiently.

2   In order to improve public health, governments should require food manufacturers to add nutrients to their products.

3   The problem of rising levels of obesity in many parts of the world is mainly due to people's lack of knowledge about food and nutrition.

4   Because fast food is generally unhealthy, governments should regulate the fast food industry in the same way that they regulate the alcohol and tobacco industries.

5   Convenience food will become increasingly prevalent and eventually replace traditional foods and traditional methods of food preparation.

6   When you write your essay, you must give reasons for your opinions. You should also show that you have 'tested' your opinion by comparing it with at least one other opinion and examined the reasoning behind it. Look at the two opinions below and the reasons a–g. Indicate which reasons support each opinion by writing letters a–g in the spaces provided. The first one has been done for you.

1   Some people strongly agree that we should return to more natural methods of food production, such as organic farming, even if this means that we produce food less efficiently. They believe this because: _c_ , ____, ____

2   Other people strongly disagree that we should return to more natural methods of food production, such as organic farming, even if this means that we produce food less efficiently. They believe this because: ____, ____, ____, ____

Reasons

a   More people will need to be employed on farms, and fewer people will be available to do work that will help the country develop economically.

b   Producing food less efficiently could lead to food shortages.

c   It is better for the environment to produce food using fewer chemicals such as pesticides and herbicides.

d   Organically produced food is no more nutritious than food produced using pesticides and artificial fertilisers.

e   Naturally produced food tastes better than food produced using more artificial methods.

f   Food that has been produced without preservatives is less likely to stay fresh, so more food may be wasted.

g   Man-made chemicals used in modern methods of food production could be harmful to human health.

> **Exam tip:** Templates are useful for training yourself to think of a range of points quickly and write about them in an organised way. However, during the actual exams, you should spend only 3–4 minutes on this stage, so you will probably have to do your preparation in your head rather than on paper.

7 Templates A and B below can be used for essay questions that involve writing about solutions to problems. Read the essay questions 1 and 2 and complete Templates A and B with the missing information a–h below.

> **1** What can governments do to encourage children to eat a healthier diet?

Template A: 'What is the solution?' essay questions			
What are the possible solutions?	**What specific action can be taken?**	**What are the positive consequences?**	**What are the drawbacks?**
1 Regulate the food industry.	Require food producers to fortify their products with vitamins.	1 _____	This would be unpopular & expensive for food producers.
2 Regulate school meals.	2 _____	Children would have at least 1 healthy meal per day.	This would not stop children from bringing unhealthy packed lunches or going out for lunch to fast food outlets.
3 3 _____	Require schools to teach children to cook healthy foods.	Children can take pride in their learning & transfer these skills to the home.	4 _____

a Schools may not have the facilities to teach cooking.
b Children would eat healthier food without having to change their habits.
c Require schools to provide only healthy food and drink at lunch time.
d Educate children about healthy eating.

> **2** Should the government regulate the fast food industry in the same way that it regulates the drug, alcohol and tobacco industries?

Template B: 'Evaluate the solution' essay questions			
What are the possible solutions?	**What specific action can be taken?**	**Positive consequence(s)**	**Drawback(s)**
Solution in the question: Regulate the fast food industry like drug, alcohol & tobacco industries.	Restrict opening hours. Restrict location, e.g. not near schools.	Send a clear signal that fast food is bad for health. 5 _____	This would not stop people cooking & eating unhealthy food at home. 6 _____
Other possible solution: public health campaign explaining the dangers of eating too much fast food	television advertising showing long-term consequences of unhealthy diet	Help people change their eating habits fundamentally. 7 _____	People could ignore government advice. 8 _____

e Reduces people's access to unhealthy foods.
f Effectiveness of public health campaigns can be difficult to measure.
g Allows freedom of choice.
h Too much government interference is unpopular with business & bad for the economy.

8   Similar templates can be used for Task 2 essay questions that require you to discuss ideas. However, instead of listing 'positive consequences' and 'drawbacks', you will list 'evidence for the idea' and 'evidence against'.

Read the essay questions 1 and 2 and complete Templates C and D with the missing information.

> 1   Dieting to lose weight has become increasingly prevalent in the developed world. Why do you think people nowadays are so concerned with body shape and size?

Template C: 'Discuss your ideas' essay questions			
	What are your ideas?	**What is the evidence for?**	**What is the evidence against?**
1	Advertisements encourage people to value slim figures.	Advertisements often show desirable consumer products alongside slim models.	Advertisers wouldn't use slim models unless the public already had a favourable view of them.
2	People associate slimness with positive character traits.	People who do not eat too much are seen as having good self-control.	1 _____
3	2 _____	3 _____	If people diet too much, they may become malnourished.

> 2   The problem of obesity is mainly due to people's lack of knowledge about healthy eating. To what extent do you agree with the statement above?

Template D: 'Evaluate an idea' essay questions		
What are the ideas?	**What is the evidence for?**	**What is the evidence against?**
Idea in the question: Obesity is due to lack of knowledge about healthy eating.	4 _____	5 _____
Other possible idea: 6 _____	7 _____	8 _____

Part 3:   Exam practice

WRITING TASK 1

You should spend about 20 minutes on this task.

The graph shows the percentage of UK adolescents following a vegetarian diet.

Summarise the information by selecting and reporting the main features.

Write at least 150 words.

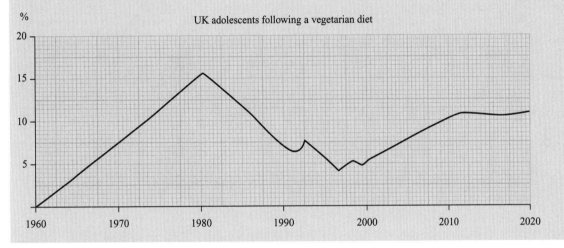

WRITING TASK 2

You should spend about 40 minutes on this task.

Write about the following topic:

Convenience foods will become increasingly prevalent and eventually replace traditional foods and traditional methods of food preparation.

To what extent do you agree or disagree with this opinion?

Give reasons for your answer and include any relevant examples from your own knowledge or experience.

Write at least 250 words.

3 Educational goals

Part 1: Vocabulary

1 Match the school subjects a–h with the pictures 1–8 above.

a Mathematics _____
b Biology _____
c Chemistry _____
d Art and Design _____

e Media, Film and Television Studies _____
f Physical Education (PE) _____
g Health and Food Technology (HFT) _____
h Computing _____

2 Each adjective in column 1 commonly collocates with one of the nouns in column 2. Complete the sentences 1–6 with one adjective and one noun.

Adjectives	Nouns
rote	standards
critical	education
higher	*dishonesty*
academic	assessment
continuous	learning
formal	thinking
educational	examinations

Example: *Cheating in examinations is one form of <u>academic dishonesty</u>.*

1 If you need to memorise large amounts of information, _____ is probably a good method to use.

2 If you need to evaluate information, you need _____ skills.

3 In many countries, students sit _____ in order to graduate.

4 Access to _____ is often determined by performance in university entrance examinations.

5 In some countries, progress is measured by _____ instead of by end-of-term examinations.

6 Some people worry that without examinations, _____ will decline.

3 **The expressions i–vi are useful for describing quantity. Match them with the percentages a–f below.**

i nearly half _____	a 85%
ii the vast majority _____	b 75%
iii a small minority _____	c 46%
iv three quarters _____	d 31%
v just under a third _____	e 24%
vi roughly one in four _____	f 15%

4 **The bar chart below shows the results of a survey of how people felt about examinations. Complete the sentences 1–6, which describe the chart, using the expressions i–vi from Exercise 3.**

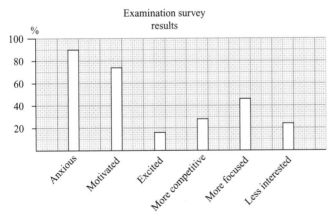

Examination survey results

1 _____ of those surveyed said they found the challenge exciting.

2 _____ of respondents said they felt anxious.

3 _____ said they felt more competitive.

4 _____ of those surveyed replied that they felt more focused.

5 _____ indicated that examinations made them lose interest in their studies.

6 _____ of those who responded said they felt motivated to work harder.

Part 2:   Practice exercises: Task 1

1   The bar chart below shows the numbers of students sitting examinations in eight different subjects and the percentage of students gaining top marks. For this type of data, you are expected not just to describe, but also to compare and contrast the information.

You can use comparative forms to compare two or more items:

- ***more/fewer/less* + noun + *than***
  Overall, <u>more students</u> sat examinations in science-related subjects <u>than</u> in arts-related subjects.
- **adjectives of one syllable: *-er* + *than***
  A <u>higher percentage</u> of students gained top marks in Mathematics than in Chemistry.
- ***more/less* + adjective of two or more syllables + *than***
  Science-related subjects were <u>more popular than</u> arts-related subjects.
  You can use superlative forms to compare one item with the remainder of the group:
- ***the most/least* + adjective**
  The <u>most popular</u> subject was Mathematics.
- **adjectives of more than one syllable: *-est***
  The <u>highest</u> percentage of students gaining top marks was in Mathematics.
  You can use *as* + adjective + *as* to express similarity: *Art and Design was nearly <u>as popular as</u> Chemistry.*

Complete the sentences 1–6 with a comparative or superlative form.

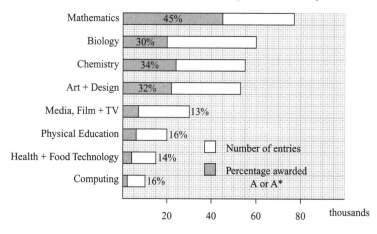

1   Nearly _____ many students sat the Art and Design exam _____ did the Chemistry exam.

2   The percentage of students gaining top marks in Art and Design was slightly _____ than the percentage of students achieving top marks in Chemistry.

3   The _____ popular subjects were Physical Education, Health and Food Technology, and Computing.

4   The HFT examination was taken by _____ students than the PE examination.

5   However, a _____ percentage of students taking the HFT exam gained top marks.

6   The _____ percentage of students gaining top marks was in Media, Film and Television Studies.

> **Exam tip:** Use adverbs to make your comparisons more exact.
> **To emphasise a difference, you can use:** *many, much, far,* and *significantly.*
> *Many* more students sat examinations in science subjects.
> *Science-related subjects were* <u>much</u> *more popular than arts-related subjects.*
>
> **For small differences you can use:** *slightly* or *nearly as … as.*
> *The percentage of students gaining top marks in Chemistry was* <u>slightly</u> *higher than the percentage of students gaining top marks in Art and Design.*
> <u>Nearly</u> *as many students sat the Art and Design exam as did the Chemistry exam.*

2 You can use expressions such as *in contrast* to express difference, or *the same* to express similarity. Read the sentences 1–4 below. Write **S** if the sentence expresses similarity and **D** if it expresses difference. Underline the words which helped you decide.

1 The percentage of top marks was quite high in subjects such as Mathematics, which are traditionally regarded as difficult. On the other hand, the percentage of top marks was relatively low in subjects such as HFT, which are commonly regarded as 'soft'. _____

2 Whereas 45 per cent of Mathematics candidates gained top marks, only 12 per cent of Media, Film and Television candidates gained top marks. _____

3 Similar numbers of students sat examinations in Art and Design and in Chemistry. _____

4 Sixteen per cent of students gained top marks in both Physical Education and Computing. _____

3 To do well in IELTS Writing Tasks, you must show that you can use a range of expressions and structures for functions like comparing and contrasting. Re-write the sentences 1–5 using the words in brackets.

1 More girls than boys passed their English examinations. (fewer)

_____

2 The same number of boys and girls achieved a passing grade in Mathematics. (as … as)

_____

3 Boys did well in Technology; girls, in contrast, did well in language-related subjects. (whereas) _____

4 The number of passes in Religious Studies was higher for girls than for boys. (lower)

_____

5 Nearly as many girls as boys passed the Economics exam. (similar)

_____

Part 2: Practice exercises: Task 2

4   Read the Task 2 question below.

> *In order to be truly employable, the educated person should be able to demonstrate not just knowledge but also the ability to work independently in teams.*
>
> *How can teamwork best be encouraged and assessed in educational settings?*

Once you have analysed the question, taken a position and generated some ideas, you need to decide which of your ideas to include and in what order to include them. You can use an essay outline to do this. Look at the example below and answer questions 1–4.

Ideas

	Solutions	Specific action	Positive consequences	Drawbacks
1	require students to work on group projects outside school	assign group research project investigating aspect of local history	• motivating for students • students would learn to work as a team • students would make more friends	• difficult to assess individual students' contribution to team • some projects would be poor quality
2	group project could be done partly in school, partly outside school	ask students to periodically present 'work in progress' in class	• teacher could monitor students' work more easily • it's better for students to be in classrooms because that's what people expect	• some teachers wouldn't be good at this • time-consuming for large classes
3	some teacher monitoring + student self-assessment	students keep a learning journal throughout the project	• burden of monitoring and assessing progress shared by teacher and students	• some students would dishonestly claim they worked harder than they did

Essay outline
Introduction: importance of training students in teamwork
Body paragraph 1:
Solution 1: require students to work on group projects outside of school
Specific action: assign group research project investigating aspect of local history
Positive consequences: motivating for students; students would learn to work as a team independently
Drawback: difficult to assess individual student's contribution to team effort
Body paragraph 2:
Solution 2: group project could be done partly in school, partly outside of school
Specific action: ask students to periodically present 'work in progress' in class
Positive consequences: teacher could monitor students' work more easily
Drawback: time-consuming for large classes

Body paragraph 3:
Solution 3: in addition to some teacher monitoring, students assess own progress
Specific action: students write a learning journal throughout the project
Positive consequences: burden of monitoring and assessing progress shared by teacher and students
Conclusion: teamwork can be taught and assessed but needs to be done in the right way

1 What type of question is this: **A**: propose a solution, **B**: evaluate a solution, **C**: present an idea or **D**: evaluate an idea?

2 Which of her ideas has the writer omitted from body paragraphs one and two? Why?

3 Why has the writer chosen to list her main ideas in this order?

4 Why has the writer included drawbacks in body paragraphs one and two but not in three?

5 Read the Task 2 question below and complete the table with your own ideas. Take a position. Then select the most appropriate ideas and write an outline using the headings given.

> Success in formal 'pen and paper' examinations is often seen to be a sign of intelligence.
>
> To what extent do you agree with the view that formal examinations measure intelligence?

Ideas

Template D: Evaluate an idea		
What are the ideas?	What is the evidence for?	What is the evidence against?
Idea in the question: Exams measure intelligence.	People who do well in exams often do well in other types of tasks, e.g. assignments. Exams usually include a range of tasks to measure different abilities.	Pen & paper exams are often predictable – students can prepare by rote learning. 1 _____ _____
Other possible idea: There are probably different types of intelligence – these can only be measured in different ways.	Some people express themselves much better verbally than in writing. 2 _____ _____	3 _____ _____ _____

Essay outline
Introduction:
Body paragraph 1:
Evidence for:
Evidence against:
Body paragraph 2:
Evidence against:
Evidence for:
Conclusion:

6   Read the Task 2 question below and complete the table with your own ideas. Take a position, select the most appropriate ideas, and write an outline.

> *In many countries, students attend private 'cram schools' for extra coaching in test-taking techniques.*
>
> *What is your view of this practice?*

Ideas

Template B: 'Evaluate the solution' essay questions		
What are the possible solutions?	**Positive consequence(s)**	**Drawback(s)**
Solution in the question:		
Other possible solution:		

Essay outline

Introduction:

Body paragraph 1:

Body paragraph 2:

Conclusion:

7   Look at Template C 'Discuss your ideas' in Unit 2. Draw up headings for an outline for this type of question.

Introduction:

Body paragraph 1:

Body paragraph 2:

Conclusion:

Part 3: Exam practice

WRITING TASK 1

You should spend about 20 minutes on this task.

> *The graph compares the percentage of international and the percentage of UK students gaining second class degrees or better at a major UK university.*
>
> *Summarise the information by selecting and reporting the main features.*

Write at least 150 words.

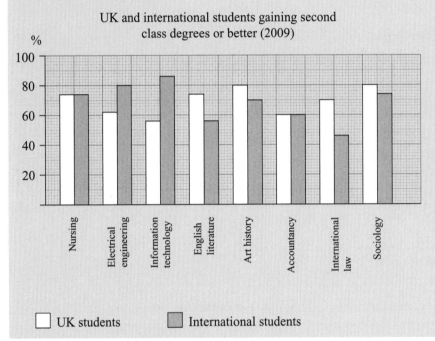

UK and international students gaining second class degrees or better (2009)

☐ UK students   ▨ International students

WRITING TASK 2

You should spend about 40 minutes on this task.

Write about the following topic:

> *Many people believe that formal 'pen and paper' examinations are not the best method of assessing educational achievement.*
>
> *What is your view of examinations?*

Give reasons for your answer and include any relevant examples from your own knowledge or experience.

Write at least 250 words.

4 Biodiversity

Aims: Describing a process | Using the active and passive voice
Signposting a sequence of events | Using the language of cause and effect
Overviewing the academic style

Part 1: Vocabulary

1 Match the pictures 1–6 above with the natural habitats a–f.

a	estuary	**c**	mangrove swamp	**e**	grasslands
b	forest	**d**	desert	**f**	rainforest

2 The expressions a–g below describe sources of damage to the environment. Complete the sentences 1–7 using these expressions. The first one has been done for you.

a	oil spills	**d**	logging	**f**	overgrazing
b	*intensive farming*	**e**	acid rain	**g**	global warming
c	strip mining				

1 *Intensive farming* in wheat-growing countries like Canada has led to the loss of natural grasslands.

2 _____ causes damage to forests as well as limestone monuments.

3 Indiscriminate _____ of tropical hardwoods has contributed to the destruction of rainforests.

4 _____ of grasslands by cattle and sheep is associated with soil erosion and desertification.

5 Off-shore _____ frequently result in damage to mangrove swamps and the unique species that live there.

6 The thinning of the arctic icecap has been attributed to _____.

7 _____ for minerals near river banks is linked to soil erosion and degradation of estuaries.

3 Look again at sentences 1–7 in exercise 2 and answer the questions 1–3.

1 Which sentences express a cause-and-effect relationship?

2 Which sentences express an association (possibly, but not necessarily, cause-and-effect)?

3 How is *contribute to* different from *cause*?

4 Cause-and-effect relationships can also be expressed using a number of different words and expressions:

because + **dependant clause**

Because mangrove swamps have been damaged, many unique species are now endangered.
Many unique species are now endangered because mangrove swamps have been damaged.

because of + **noun phrase**
Because of damage to mangrove swamps, many unique species are now endangered.

due to
Many unique species are now endangered due to damage to mangrove swamps.

therefore/consequently/as a result + **clause**
Mangrove swamps have been damaged; therefore, many unique species are now endangered.

so
Mangrove swamps have been damaged, so many unique species are now endangered.

so + ***that*** + **clause**
Mangrove swamps have been so damaged that many unique species are now endangered.

Re-write the sentences 1–4 below using the words in brackets. Make any other changes necessary.

1 Land has been farmed so intensively that there has been a significant decline in biodiversity. (contributed to)
Intensive farming _____.

2 Loss of vegetation has caused a decline in the insect population. (consequently)
Vegetation _____.

3 Because there are fewer insects, the small animals that feed on them have moved elsewhere. (so)
There are _____.

4 The disappearance of prey species has resulted in a marked reduction in numbers of predators such as wild cats and owls. (because of)
There has been _____.

5 Each pair of words or phrases in italics in the sentences 1–5 below expresses a similar meaning. Underline the word which makes the sentence more moderate.

1 Acid rain has *damaged/destroyed* acres of forest.

2 As a result, many woodland species *have become extinct/are endangered*.

3 The *loss/disappearance* of predator species has caused an increase in numbers of prey species.

4 Many forests can no longer be *used/exploited* for commercial purposes.

5 Governments should *ban/limit* the burning of fossil fuels, which causes acid rain.

Part 2: Practice exercises: Task 1

1 Read the two process descriptions below. Use information from the second description to complete the flowchart.

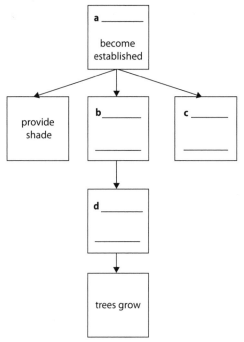

Clear cutting

The flow chart illustrates the process of clear cutting, a logging practice which involves the complete removal of trees from a given area.

Firstly, access roads to the area are cut. Secondly, the entire crop of standing trees is felled by mechanized harvesters. The trees are then 'extracted', or brought to the road side.

Once the trees have been extracted, they are processed by chain saw. The limbs and tree tops are removed. The stems are 'bucked', that is cut into logs of a specified length. The logs are then sorted by size and loaded onto logging trucks for transport to the sawmill.

In the final stage, the land is prepared for future harvests. The remaining scrub is gathered into large piles and burnt. The area is then re-planted.

Forest re-growth

The flowchart illustrates the process of forest re-growth following a period of widespread deforestation.

The first plants to grow are 'pioneer' plants, which can survive in harsh conditions. They provide shade, gather moisture, and return organic material to the soil. They therefore create the conditions for other plants to thrive.

In the second phase of re-growth, shrubs emerge. They quickly cover the ground, crowding out the pioneers. However, they too eventually die off as young trees push through the brush. Within ten years, trees finally take over, preventing light from reaching the forest floor.

Now look at options **i** and **ii** and decide in each case whether you would normally use the active or the passive voice.

i   when the process is natural
ii when there is a human agent

2   The descriptions on page 34 contain examples of how several stages of a process can be combined in one sentence. Read the descriptions again and notice how the groups of sentences 1–5 below have been combined. Study the examples and then join each group of sentences without looking at the model texts. The first one has been done for you.

Example: *The first plants to grow are pioneer plants. Pioneer plants can survive in harsh conditions.*
The first plants to grow are pioneer plants, which can survive in harsh conditions.

1   Pioneer plants provide shade. Pioneer plants gather moisture. Pioneer plants return organic material to the soil.

_____

2   Shrubs quickly cover the ground. Shrubs crowd out the pioneers.

_____

3   However, shrubs too eventually die off. Young trees push through the brush.

_____

4   The logs are sorted by size. The logs are loaded onto logging trucks. They are transported to the sawmill.

_____

5   The trees have been extracted. The trees are processed by chain saw.

_____

3   The descriptions in Exercise 1 also contain examples of **signposting** language, which mark the stages of the process. Find examples from the texts in Exercise 1 that signpost the following stages:

beginning stages: *Firstly*

middle stages:

end stages:

> **Exam tip:** Do not overuse signposting expressions. One signposting expression at the start, one or two in the middle and one at the end are sufficient in most cases. In process descriptions, the most frequently used signpost is the adverb *then*. It is normally placed between the subject and verb (*Precipitation then increases*) or between the auxiliary verb and the main verb (*The trees are then extracted*).

4   The process diagram below includes both man-made and natural phenomena. Complete the sentences 1–10 using an active or passive verb form. The first one has been done for you.

1 A dam *is constructed* at the river head.

2 The flow of water _____ down.

3 Flooding _____ less frequent.

4 A sand bar _____ across the estuary.

5 The quantity of nutrients on land declines and agricultural output _____.

6 Salinity in the estuary _____.

7 The human population _____.

8 Fewer fish _____.

9 Mangrove trees _____.

10 Mangrove cover in the estuary _____.

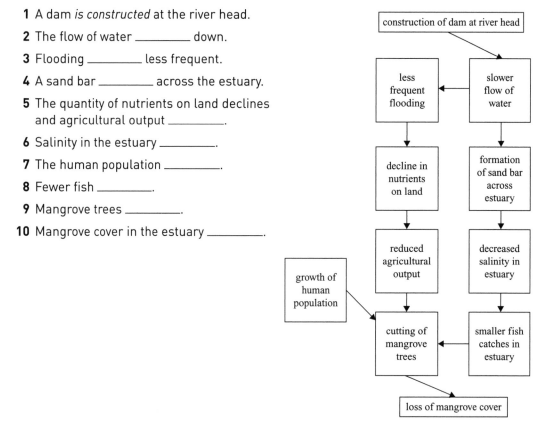

5   Join each pair of sentences a–f below using the structure, word or expression in brackets. Make any other necessary changes. Then rewrite the sentences as a passage, adding any signposting expressions from Exercise 3 that you think are suitable.

a   1 and 2 (-*ing* clause) Example: *A dam is constructed at the river head, slowing the flow of water.*

b   3 and 5 (because)   _____

c   4 and 6 (as a result)   _____

d   6 and 8 (as)   _____

e   7, 8 and 9 (due to)   _____

f   9 and 10 (once)   _____

Part 2: Practice exercises: Task 2

6 Compare the introductions and first body paragraphs of two responses to the Task 2 question below. Underline the differences and then answer questions 1–2.

> *Many species of plants and animals have come and gone throughout the history of the Earth. From this perspective, extinction can be seen as part of a natural process. Some people have argued that we should not, therefore, make heroic efforts to preserve the natural habitats of endangered plants and animals when doing so would conflict with human interests.*
>
> *To what extent do you agree with this view?*

Response 1

If you look at it that way, it's true that humans and animals have conflicting interests. People have always exploited animals for food and clothing, and farmers have brought bigger and bigger areas of land under cultivation. But should we keep on doing this?

In regions of the world where the population is growing, and there aren't enough resources, the conflict between humans and animals is really bad. If you go to Africa, for example, you can see large nature reserves alongside really poor human settlements. I love the idea of elephants and lions living in the wild. But often it's the poor farmer living nearby who's got to pay the cost in terms of land and lost earnings.

Response 2

Looked at from a broad historical perspective, it is true that humans and animals have conflicting interests. People have always exploited animals for food and clothing, whilst farmers have brought ever-increasing areas of land under cultivation. Whether this process should continue is a question that requires careful consideration.

In regions of the world where the population is growing, and resources are scarce, the conflict between humans and animals is particularly problematic. This can be seen in parts of Africa, for example, where large nature reserves sit alongside very poor human settlements. People living thousands of miles away may value the idea of elephants and lions living in the wild. However, often it is the poor farmer living nearby who must pay the cost in terms of land and lost earnings.

1 What is the main difference between these two responses?

2 What are the main characteristics of the style of the second response?

7 The table on page 38 outlines four characteristics of academic style. Complete the table with examples from the texts in Exercise 6.

> **Exam tip:** If writing in an academic style is new to you, make sure that you do not write in an overly complicated way. Above all, your writing should be clear and easy to read. Avoid writing more than one subordinate clause in each complex sentence. Do not write in a way that is so impersonal that your message is obscured. Do not use a lot of words to express an idea when a few words would be sufficient.

Characteristics of academic style	Examples from Responses 1 and 2	
	Informal style	Academic style
Academic style is impersonal. Avoid overusing personal pronouns (e.g. *I, you, we*) and addressing the reader directly.	*If you look at it that way, ...*	*Looked at from a broad historical perspective, ...*
Academic style is not emotional. Avoid absolute statements and exaggeration (e.g. *totally, perfect*), emotive words (e.g. *terrible, adore*) and words that express value judgments (e.g. *immoral*).	*bad*	*problematic*
Academic style uses fewer conjunctions (*and, but*) and more subordinators (*whereas, because*) and sentence linkers (*nevertheless, therefore*).	*and farmers*	*whilst farmers*
Academic style uses different vocabulary. Avoid colloquial expressions, phrasal verbs (e.g. *take up, break out*), double comparatives (e.g. *more and more*), contacted forms (e.g. *isn't, won't*) and the words *get, a lot of* and *really*.	*It's*	*It is*

8 **Re-write the second half of the essay below in the academic style.**

But if you think about plants, the advantages of conservation are more apparent. You have to remember that wild plants aren't just things of beauty; they're also a really valuable resource. Wild plants have been used throughout history to make medicines. Take aspirin, for example. And if certain varieties of crops are prone to disease, you could use wild plants to develop new varieties. There are lots of plants that we haven't even discovered yet, so you never know what they might be useful for.

All in all, I'd say it's worth trying to preserve natural habitats because wild animals and plants are really special and they could be life savers. But we've got to remember that people's basic needs have to be met too. So, we have to do it in a fair way.

9 **Re-write the sentences 1–2 below to make them clearer and easier to read. Remove unnecessary words and divide long sentences if required.**

Example: *The desirability of avoiding environmental degradation is an idea that most people probably agree with.*

Most people do not want to damage the environment.

1 It could be argued, though the opposite view might be equally true, that the tendency that many people have to acquire riches and material wealth is one of several possible factors that may encourage people to exploit the natural environment excessively.

2 It is possible that some people may believe that environmental degradation is a process that cannot be avoided in the long term because the countries of the world do not have a way or means of enforcing environmental agreements which their leaders may have committed themselves to, possibly for the wrong reasons, for instance simply to create a favourable impression in the mass media and television.

Part 3: Exam practice

WRITING TASK 1

You should spend about 20 minutes on this task.

> The flow chart illustrates the consequences of deforestation.
>
> Summarise the information by selecting and reporting the main features.

Write at least 150 words.

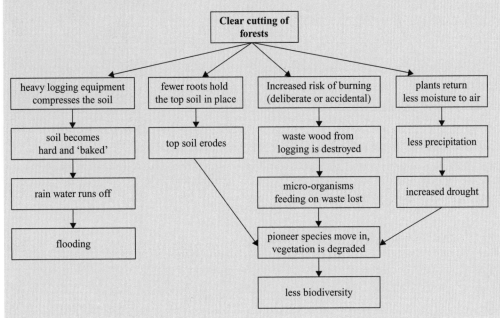

WRITING TASK 2

You should spend about 40 minutes on this task.

Write about the following topic:

> The importance of biodiversity is being more widely recognised as increasing numbers of species come under threat.
>
> What can be done to maintain biodiversity?

Give reasons for your answer and include any relevant examples from your own knowledge or experience.

Write at least 250 words.

5 Global English

Part 1: Vocabulary

1 The expressions a–h below are all related to language.
Use each expression once to complete the sentences 1–8.

a bilingual
b foreign language
c lingua franca
d minority languages

e mother tongue
f non-native
g official language
h standard form

1 The majority of people living in the US, the UK, Canada, Australia, and New Zealand speak English as their _____.

2 English is a(n) _____ in a further fifty-three countries, including India and the Philippines.

3 English is the most widely taught _____ in the world.

4 Because English is used by so many people around the world for so many purposes, it is widely regarded as a _____.

5 The ratio of _____ speakers to native speakers of English is roughly three to one.

6 People who can speak two languages fluently are commonly referred to as _____.

7 There are many different varieties of English spoken throughout the world; in fact, there is no single _____.

8 Many people fear that the spread of English as a global language will contribute to the death of _____.

2 Match the types of words and expressions 1–7 below with the examples a–g.

1 a loanword	a lol
2 a colloquialism	b thou
3 a dialect of English	c café
4 a technical term	d There's more than one way to skin a cat.
5 an obsolete term	e Geordie
6 a saying	f wanna (= 'want to')
7 text speak	g refraction

3 In IELTS Writing Task 2, you are often required to express more than one point of view. You can use reporting verbs to do this. In English, there is a wide variety of reporting verbs, which can be used:
- to express beliefs: *believe, maintain, suspect, think*
- in discussion: *argue, assert, claim, insist, say*
- to show agreement: *accept, acknowledge, admit, advocate, agree, concede, support*
- to show disagreement: *challenge, deny, disagree, dismiss, doubt, object, question, refute*
- to give suggestions: *imply, suggest, urge*

Reporting verbs can be tentative (e.g. *suspect, suggest*), neutral (e.g. *say, agree*), or emphatic (e.g. *assert, dismiss*). Look at the sentences 1–7 below and underline the stronger of the two reporting verbs.

1 Many people *insist/argue* that there is one 'best' variety of English.

2 However, I *question/refute* the idea that one variety of the language is better than another.

3 Some people *doubt/deny* the value of a bilingual education.

4 Others *accept/advocate* the idea of a bilingual education, even for very young children.

5 I would *urge/suggest that* educational authorities do all they can to promote minority languages.

6 Some people *suspect/maintain* that within a century, there will only be two or three languages spoken in the world.

7 Other people *dismiss/doubt* the idea that all but two or three languages will die out.

4 Different reporting verbs are followed by different structures:
- ***that* + clause:** *Some people argue that governments should subsidise ...*
- ***whether* + clause:** *Others question whether governments should subsidise ...*
- **reporting verb +**
  - **preposition + noun/noun phrase:** *I object to the policy of government subsidies ...*
  - **noun/noun phrase:** *Most people support the idea of subsidising ...*
  - **gerund:** *Educators recommend subsidising ...*
  - **object + infinitive verb:** *I would urge the government to subsidise ...*

Some reporting verbs can be followed by more than one type of structure. For example:
- **question +**
  - ***whether* + clause:** *Others question whether schools should promote ...*
  - **noun phrase:** *Others question the feasibility of promoting ...*

Re-write the sentences 1–4 below using the phrases a–d. Make any changes necessary for a more academic style.

a Some people insist ...	**c** I concede ...
b Teachers recommend ...	**d** I refute the idea ...

1 Maybe making English a mandatory subject in primary schools isn't such a good idea.

_____

2 The world definitely needs one common language for trade.

_____

3 It is highly unlikely that everyone in the world will speak the same language at any point in the future.

_____

4 You should practise a foreign language outside the classroom if you want to become really fluent in it.

_____

Part 2: Practice exercises: Task 1

1 Sometimes IELTS Writing Task 1 requires you to describe a diagram. Read the response below, which describes a diagram showing the relationship between a number of different languages. Sketch the diagram to see how well you understood the description.

> The diagram shows the languages of Europe, Iran, and the Indian subcontinent and how they are related through a common Indo-European root language.
>
> There are seven main branches: three represent the languages spoken throughout Western Europe, and four represent the languages spoken further to the east. The Western European branches include the Celtic, Germanic, and Italic languages. Some of these languages, such as Scots or Welsh, are spoken by relatively few people, but others, including German and English (from the Germanic branch) and French and Spanish (Italic branch) are among the most widely spoken languages in the world.
>
> The eastern Indo-European branches include the languages spoken in Iran, the Indian Subcontinent, Greece, and the Slavic countries. The Indian branch comprises several languages including Hindi, Urdu and Bengali. The Slavic branch covers languages spoken in Eastern Europe, such as Russian and Polish, as well as Czech.
>
> Overall, the diagram shows that languages that are commonly regarded as very different are, in fact, related.

2 Look at the diagram below and the text on page 43 which describes it. Put the paragraphs a–d in the correct order. Then answer the questions 1–4.

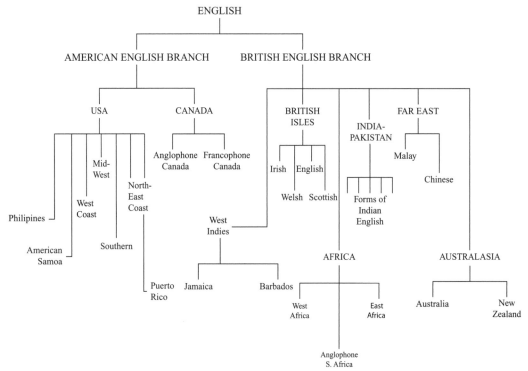

a The American branch is largely restricted to the American continent. It comprises the varieties of English spoken in the different regions of the United States itself, as well as in Canada. Beyond the continent, the extent of its influence is limited to the Philippines in the Far East and American Samoa in the Pacific.

b In brief, the diagram shows that, like the economic and political influence of the Anglo-Saxon countries, the reach of English has extended to virtually every region of the world.

c The diagram shows the varieties of English spoken throughout the world and how they are related.

d There are two main branches of English: British English and American English. The British English Branch is geographically wide-spread. It extends across several continents from the West Indies, through the British Isles themselves, Africa, the Indian subcontinent, the Far East and Australasia. In addition to the four varieties of English spoken in the British Isles (i.e. in Ireland, Wales, Scotland and England), it includes a large number of other varieties, for instance Jamaican English, South African English, and Australian English.

1 Which paragraphs refer to the whole diagram and which paragraphs refer to parts of the diagram?

2 How is the introduction different from the conclusion?

3 Do the body paragraphs give general information first and then specific information, or vice versa?

4 Which expressions from the text would you learn because they will be useful when writing about categories and classifications?

3 **Look at the Task 1 instructions below. Then read the sentences a–d and answer the questions 1–3.**

> *The diagram illustrates the percentage of the world population that speaks minority, mid-sized, and dominant languages.*
>
> *Summarise the information by selecting and reporting the main features.*

a The diagram shows the percentage of the world population that speaks minority, mid-sized, and dominant languages.

b The diagram shows the number of languages classified as minority, mid-sized, or dominant, and the proportion of people in the world that speak them.

c The diagram shows that although many languages are spoken throughout the world, the size of their respective speech communities varies enormously.

d The diagram shows that a very small number of languages (approximately 100) hold a dominant position, whereas more than half of the world's languages are spoken by a very small percentage of the world population (0.2%).

1 Which of the sentences a–d would work well as an introduction?

2 Which would work well as a conclusion?

3 What is the problem with sentence a?

4 Why might you not want to use sentence d as an introduction or conclusion?

4   **Complete the introductory and the concluding sentences for the figure below.**

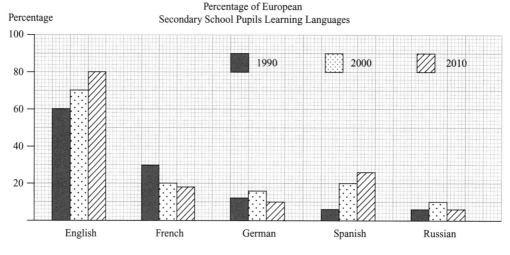

Percentage of European
Secondary School Pupils Learning Languages

1   Introduction:
    The bar chart shows ...

2   Conclusion:
    In summary, ...

Part 2: Practice exercises: Task 2

5   In introductions to academic essays, writers often:

     a   state the topic of the essay: *This essay is about ...*

     b   write something about the general context: *In recent years ...*

     c   explain why the topic is interesting, relevant or important: *X is interesting/relevant/ important because*

     d   present a viewpoint that they go on to challenge: *Some people believe that ...*

     e   present their own viewpoint: *In my view, ...*

     f   state the purpose of the essay: *The aim of this essay is to ...*

     g   outline the structure of the essay: *This essay will firstly ..., secondly ..., thirdly ...*

Read the Task 2 question below and the introduction that follows. For each section of the introduction, indicate which of the functions a–g above is being addressed. Then answer the questions 1–2.

> *As the English language becomes more widespread, some speakers of other languages fear that English loanwords are gradually replacing perfectly adequate native words.*
>
> *To what extent do you believe that people should seek to protect the 'purity' of their language from the influence of English?*

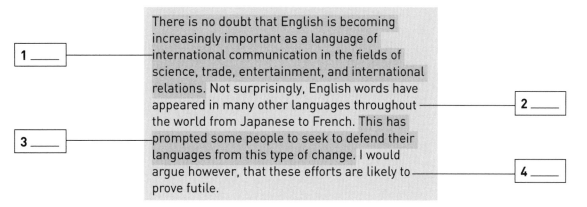

1 ____

2 ____

3 ____

4 ____

There is no doubt that English is becoming increasingly important as a language of international communication in the fields of science, trade, entertainment, and international relations. Not surprisingly, English words have appeared in many other languages throughout the world from Japanese to French. This has prompted some people to seek to defend their languages from this type of change. I would argue however, that these efforts are likely to prove futile.

     1   How would you describe the overall organisation of the introductory paragraph? Does it begin with the writer's opinion and then explain the context, or vice versa?

     2   Why has the writer presented his/her own view last?

6   Read the Task 2 question below and the sentences 1–5 on page 46. For each sentence, indicate its function a–g, listed in Exercise 5 above. Then arrange the sentences in the most effective order.

> *With regard to foreign language learning, the effectiveness of out-of-class learning is well-established. What are the best ways of learning a foreign language outside of a classroom situation?*

1 I believe the success of out-of-class learning suggests that not all language learning needs to be classroom-based. _____

2 However, in many cases, additional languages are learned not in the classroom, but through exposure to a language in day-to-day activities. _____

3 Around the world, people who speak only their mother tongue are probably outnumbered by those who speak one or more additional languages. _____

4 In this essay, I will outline what I believe to be the three most effective ways of independent language learning. _____

5 Many people assume that the classroom is the best place to learn a foreign language. _____

> **Exam tip:** Academic writing values modesty and tolerance of others' views. Therefore, when expressing your opinion, it is often more effective to use the more tentative or neutral reporting verbs. Rather than writing: *I insist that governments do more to protect minority languages*, write: *I believe that governments should do more ....* Use the more emphatic verbs for expressing viewpoints that you wish to challenge: *Some people insist that there can only be one officially recognised variety of a language. I would argue, however, that no single variety should be favoured.*

7 **Complete the introduction below with the expressions a–f.**

> *Many education systems throughout the world recognise the value of learning a foreign language and are seeking to improve the way foreign languages are taught.*
>
> *What in your view is the best way of teaching a foreign language in schools and universities?*

a	right approach	**d**	the world becomes
b	the most effective methods	**e**	increasingly important
c	therefore	**f**	I will outline

As (1) _____ more integrated, the ability to speak a foreign language is becoming (2) _____, not just for individuals, but also for nations. The teaching of foreign languages is labour-intensive and (3) _____ costly, so it is important that the (4) _____ is taken. In this essay, (5) _____ what I consider to be (6) _____ of language teaching in a classroom context.

8 **Write introductions for the Task 2 questions below.**

1 As English becomes more widespread as a lingua franca, there is concern that the values and culture of the English-speaking world will displace native values and cultures. To what extent is this fear justified?

2 Sometimes misunderstandings occur among people from different cultures, even those who can communicate in a common language. What factors can contribute to the breakdown of cross-cultural communication?

Part 3: Exam practice

WRITING TASK 1

You should spend about 20 minutes on this task.

> *The diagram shows the main systems of writing used throughout the world.*
>
> *Summarise the information by selecting and reporting the main features.*

Write at least 150 words.

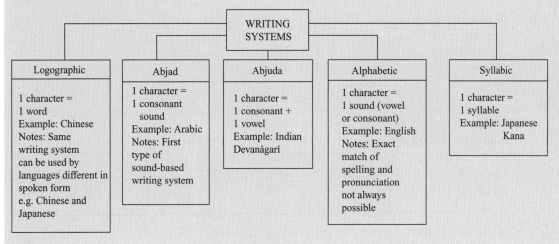

WRITING TASK 2

You should spend about 40 minutes on this task.

Write about the following topic:

> *As languages such as English, Spanish and Mandarin become more widely spoken, there is a fear that many minority languages may die out. Some countries have taken steps to protect minority languages.*
>
> *What is your view of this practice?*

Give reasons for your answer and include any relevant examples from your own knowledge or experience.

Write at least 250 words.

6   The Internet

Part 1:   Vocabulary

1   What are the a–f activities below called when you do them online? Match them to the images 1–6 above.

   a   accessing the news   **d**   online banking
   b   downloading films   **e**   searching for information
   c   Internet shopping   **f**   social networking

2   In IELTS Writing Tasks, it is important to highlight key points. The words a–f below can be used to do this. Match them with the correct definitions i–vi.

a distinctive	i affecting many people or places
b main	ii easy to see
c noticeable	iii important
d significant	iv most important
e underlying	v real and basic but not obvious
f widespread	vi unique, special or characteristic

3 Complete the sentences 1–5 with the best adjective from Exercise 2.
Notice how they form common collocations with the nouns in italics.

Example: *There was a <u>significant</u> correlation between age and number of hours spent gaming online.*

1 At first glance, the most _____ *change* was in the growing popularity of social networking; however, on closer examination, it is clear that other changes were more fundamental.

2 The graph shows that the spread of wireless technology has a _____ regional *pattern*. In fact, this pattern is characteristic of the spread of new technology generally.

3 While there was some variation in the use of online auction sites, the _____ *trend* has been upward.

4 Although price is undoubtedly a factor, the _____ *reason* customers chose the newer mobile devices is because of their wide range of applications.

5 The _____ *distribution* of towns in that region made investment in telecommunications infrastructure worthwhile. Less populated regions attracted less investment.

4 The words in italics in the passage below are useful for writing about science- and technology-related topics. Read the text and match the words in italics a–f with the definitions 1–6.

1 arrival
2 development
3 gradual change
4 make possible
5 speeded/sped up
6 tools

It is often said that the technological (a) *advance* that had the greatest impact on everyday life in the early twentieth century was the telephone. This is not surprising given the effect (b) *devices*, such as the telephone, have had on social relationships. When first developed, the telephone was marketed as a practical tool for conducting business; however within a few decades, it was being increasingly used to meet people's emotional and social needs. This (c) *trend* has (d) *accelerated* with the (e) *advent* of a new generation of wireless devices, which (f) *enable* users to stay in touch with friends and family virtually twenty-four hours a day.

5 The paragraph below comes from an essay written in response to the Task 2 question:
Which new technology of the last fifty years has had the greatest impact on daily life?
Complete the paragraph with the correct form of the words in italics a–f in Exercise 4.

Although there have been many important technological (1) _____ over the last five decades, the (2) _____ of the Internet has probably had the most significant effect on everyday life. The Internet (3) _____ people to access more information than ever before. This (4) _____ is (5) _____ as whole libraries are being made available online. Moreover, with instant messaging and social networking, it is cheaper and more convenient to communicate with others via the Internet. Within the next decade, the Internet will probably replace the older generation of telecommunication (6) _____, such as the telephone.

Part 2: Practice exercises: Task 1

1   Study the table below which shows the percentage of time Internet users spent on the eight most popular online activities in 2007 and 2009. Compare the two responses and answer the questions 1–3.

1   Which response do you think is more satisfactory? Why?

2   Which sentences in the two responses contain main points? How are these signposted? Underline the signposting.

3   In each response, where is the detailed information in relation to the general statements?

Rank	Activity	Share of time 2007 (%)	Share of time 2009 (%)
1	Social networking	14	24
2	Watching videos	10	11
3	E-mailing	16	9
4	Instant messaging	11	6
5	Downloading music	4	5
6	Searching for information	4	4
7	Online banking	3	3
8	Accessing news	2	2
	Other	36	36

Response 1

The table shows that there were significant changes in how Internet users spent their time online over a two-year period.

The percentage of time spent on social networking sites increased sharply from fourteen per cent to twenty-four per cent. The proportion of time devoted to watching videos also increased, but only by a small amount (from ten per cent to eleven per cent). There was also a twenty per cent increase in time spent downloading music. The time spent on email, on the other hand, dipped significantly (sixteen per cent to nine per cent). This was also true of instant messaging, which fell from eleven per cent to six per cent. The other activities listed (searching for information, online banking, and accessing the news) all remained constant at four, three, and two per cent respectively.

Overall, the way that users spent their time on the Internet varied significantly, with some activities, such as social networking, becoming more popular and others becoming less popular.

Response 2

The table shows that there were significant changes in how Internet users spent their time online over a two-year period.

The most significant change was in the way users communicated online. The use of social networking increased significantly from fourteen per cent to twenty-four per cent. However, this appears to be at the expense of other forms of online communication, namely email and instant messaging, which both declined sharply to only nine per cent and six per cent respectively of total activity.

Another noticeable trend was the relatively small increase in entertainment-related activities, such as watching videos and downloading music, with each climbing one percentage point. Other activities, which can be seen as more practical, such as searching for information, online banking, and accessing the news remained constant at a relatively low four, three, and two per cent respectively.

Overall, in 2009 users continued to spend a large share of their time online interacting with others (nearly forty per cent in total); however, their preferred way of doing so had changed.

Exam tip: To find patterns in the data more easily, try grouping similar items together and looking for associated trends. If you can't see a pattern immediately, switch your focus. In the second response above, the writer started by grouping online activities into themes: communication, entertainment, practical needs. Alternatively, she could have started by grouping items according to type of change (positive, negative, or neutral) and then looked for other connections within each group.

2 Study the table below and follow steps 1–4.

1 Focus on the bottom row. What general points can you make from the data shown? Which figure seems to be the most important?

2 Now focus on the regions listed in the first column. How might you group these regions into different categories? Think about developed and developing regions.

3 Switch your focus to the percentages listed in the third column. Which regions have the largest percentages of Internet users? Which regions have the smallest? How does this information relate to the categories of regions you have identified?

4 Switch your focus again to the last column. Notice the biggest and smallest changes. How does this information relate to the information in column 3? What connections can you make?

World regions	Number of Internet users (millions)	Internet users as % of population	Growth in Internet use 2000 – 2010
Africa	109	10%	2,421%
Asia	921	24%	602%
Middle East	59	30%	1,785%
Europe	473	59%	353%
Latin America	199	33%	1,123%
North America	271	78%	137%
Australia	20	60%	181%
TOTAL	2,052	29%	455%

Exam tip: You should 'signpost' general statements, i.e. introduce them with expressions such as *The table/pie chart/graph/etc. shows ... The most significant change ... Another noticeable trend ... Overall ...* You must also support general statements with detailed information from the table/graph/etc.

3 Write three general statements about the information in the table above. Then develop each of your general statements with one or two supporting details.

Example: *The table shows that over the last ten years there has been an exponential increase in Internet use worldwide. The number of Internet users expanded nearly five-fold, with the proportion of the world's population enjoying Internet access now standing at nearly thirty per cent.*

Part 2: Practice exercises: Task 2

4　Study the Task 2 essay question and essay plan below. What are the strengths and weaknesses of this plan?

> To what extent does the Internet increase social cohesion?

Essay outline

Introduction: Internet very important in modern life; two sides to this debate

1　Internet can increase social isolation

   a　Shy teens always surfing net – losing social skills & real friends?

   b　Couple addicted to online gaming, arrested for child neglect

   c　At work spend all morning reading emails, no time for meeting – bad for teamwork?

2　However, Internet can also bring people closer together

   d　Stuck at home with injury, used net to keep in touch with friends

   e　Used net to stay in touch with family when studying abroad – phone calls too expensive

   f　Through social networking can meet friends of friends

   g　Email & instant messaging more useful than phone for collaboration if written record needed

Conclusion: Internet can create more togetherness if used in right way

5　Look at an alternative essay plan below. Write the topic sentences 2–3 by expanding the notes. Then indicate where you would place the supporting points a–g from Exercise 4 above. What are the advantages of this plan?

Essay outline

Introduction: Internet can affect how relate to family, friends, and colleagues in both good & bad ways

1　The Internet has the potential to diminish family life but also to enhance it.
Supporting points: b, ＿＿

2　Similarly, the Internet can ... friends; however, it can also ...
Supporting points: a, ＿＿, ＿＿, ＿＿, ＿＿

3　... work ...
Supporting points: ＿＿, ＿＿

Conclusion: Internet can create more togetherness if used appropriately

6   Read the sentences below and answer questions 1–2.

Excessive Internet use leads to social isolation.

Excessive Internet use can lead to social isolation.

1   Which of these sentences is more appropriate for an academic context? Why?

2   In what other ways could you modify the first sentence to make it less sweeping?

Exam tip: It is important not to make absolute or sweeping statements. You can do this by using a range of modifiers and 'softer' vocabulary.

Quantifiers:	**Verbs:**	**Frequency adverbs:**
some	*appear*	*sometimes*
many	*seem*	*often*
most	*tend*	*rarely*

Expressions:	**Modal verbs:**	**Probability adverbs:**
It is said that …	*can*	*possibly*
It is possible …	*could*	*probably*
In some circumstances …	*may*	*perhaps*

Example:
Rapid technological change destroys traditional values.
Rapid technological change can weaken traditional values.

---

7   Modify the statements 1–6 so that they are more appropriate.

1   People over the age of fifty cannot grasp new technology.

_____

2   Everyone wants to own the latest gadget.

_____

3   Children are corrupted by the Internet.

_____

4   People do not like new technology because they do not understand it.

_____

5   Too much technology makes people lazy.

_____

6   The world's problems will be solved by advances in science and technology.

_____

8   Look at the Task 2 essay question and essay plan below. The candidate has written the introductory paragraph and notes (a–i) for the question:

> *To what extent has information technology reduced social inequality?*
>
> *Give reasons for your answer and include any relevant examples from your own knowledge or experience.*

Complete the body of the essay by following steps 1–3.

Step 1: Write G next to the notes which can be expanded to form general statements and S next to those that give specific supporting information.

Step 2: Put the notes in a logical order. Think about the best sequence of general statements and make sure that each is followed by one or two supporting details.

Step 3: Write your essay and remember:

- Expand the notes into sentences.
- Add 'signposting' expressions to emphasise important points.
- If necessary, add modifiers or use 'softer' vocabulary to make statements less sweeping.

People who live in highly developed countries often take access to information technology for granted. They find it hard to imagine a world in which this technology does not bring greater prosperity. However, as the IT revolution moves forward in some parts of the world, in other parts of the world the poor are falling further and further behind. Indeed there are many barriers to wider IT access and its potential benefits.

a In some countries, fewer than 50% population able to read

b Use of blocking software & firewalls common

c Electricity supply irregular

d Government censorship of Internet widespread

e Even where IT access available, governments fearful of well-informed public

f Broadband access only in major cities

g Illiteracy a major obstacle

h Basic infrastructure inadequate

i Women & the poor especially likely to be illiterate

Part 3: Exam practice

WRITING TASK 1

You should spend about 20 minutes on this task.

> *The table shows the average length of video advertisements on the Internet and the average length of time viewers spend watching them.*
>
> *Summarise the information by selecting and reporting the main features, and make comparisons where relevant.*

Write at least 150 words.

Average online video ad length and time viewed		
Type of advertisement	Average length of advertisement (seconds)	Average time viewed (seconds)
Public service	45.8	18.5
Automotive	27.2	14.7
Financial services	20.5	16.3
Travel	18.0	13.0
Entertainment	27.8	10.8
Home furnishings	17.3	10.0
Consumer electronics	15.3	7.1
Pharmaceuticals	16.6	6.3
Clothing	14.6	6.0
Other retail	21.0	4.5
Overall	**22.4**	**10.7**

WRITING TASK 2

You should spend about 40 minutes on this task.

Write about the following topic:

> *New technologies and ways of buying and selling are transforming the lives of consumers.*
>
> *To what extent do you agree or disagree with this opinion?*

Give reasons for your answer and include any relevant examples from your own knowledge or experience.

Write at least 250 words.

7 Consumer spending

Aims: Working with two visual prompts | Making correlations
Developing supporting examples

Part 1: Vocabulary

1 Match the expressions a–h to the segments 1–8 of the pie chart below.

a food and drink

b transportation

c clothing and footwear

d entertainment

e housing

f dining out

g utilities

h home furnishings

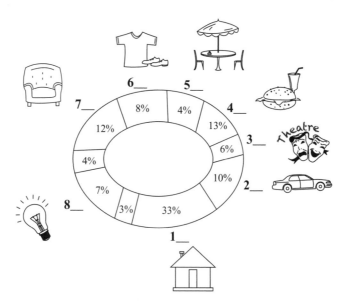

2 The words below can be paired to form common collocations. Complete the sentences 1–5 on page 57 by choosing one word from each list.

1 consumer, goods, disposable, personal, household

2 debt, expenditure, income, confidence, services

1 _____ _____ is the amount of money left after you have paid for all of the things that you need.

2 Over the last two decades, many people spent more money than they earned, resulting in high levels of _____ _____.

3 Spending on _____ and _____, such as clothing and financial advice has slowed down because of the economic crisis.

4 When people feel more secure in their jobs, _____ _____ grows and people begin to spend money more freely.

5 _____ _____ is another way of saying the amount of money each domestic unit spends.

3 Replace the words in italics in the sentences 1–6 with the more precise expressions a–f.

a their necessities
b their possessions
c aspects of

d products
e take action
f advantages

1 People often buy *things*, even when they do not need them. _____

2 One of the interesting *things about* consumer behaviour is that it is often irrational. _____

3 People can *do things* to avoid getting into debt. _____

4 One of the *good things* about shopping online is the convenience. _____

5 Often people's income barely covers the cost of *the things that they need*. _____

6 People are often very attached to *the things that they own*. _____

4 The following paragraph comes from an essay written in response to the Task 2 question: *How do people learn to manage their money?* **Complete the text with the words a–g.**

a on credit
b quantity
c financial
d criteria

e behaviour
f saved
g costly

Learning by example is one important method. From their early years, children can observe how their parents make (1) _____ decisions. They may notice, for example, whether money is (2) _____ for (3) _____ purchases, or whether purchases are bought (4) _____. Children can also see what kinds of (5) _____ parents use when choosing what to buy, for instance, whether quality or (6) _____ is more important. It is important, therefore, that parents model sensible purchasing (7) _____ and explain what they are doing and why. However, in many circumstances, this may not be sufficient.

Part 2: Practice exercises: Task 1

1   Answer the questions 1–4 in the box above in relation to the two figures below.

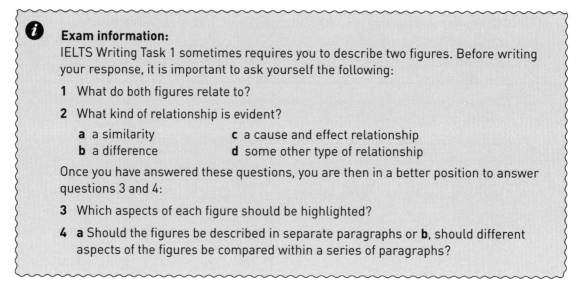

Disposable income by age (UK)

£/week

Legend: —— 15–24   ······· 35–44   ----- 65–74

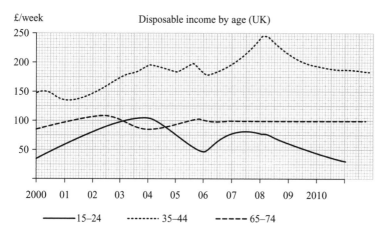

Percentage increase or decrease in sales

	2001	2004	2007	2010
Trainers	1%	5%	3%	−1%
Business suits	−2%	5%	7%	−6%
Video games	2%	6%	4%	1%
Reading glasses	0%	−1%	1%	−1%
Books	1%	4%	10%	−6%
Children's toys	1%	5%	8%	−8%

2   Read the response below and answer questions 1–6.

> The line graph shows average disposable income for three different age groups from 2000 to 2010. The table gives the percentage increase in sales for six different products at three-year intervals from 2001 to 2010. Seen together, the figures suggest a link between the disposable income of different age groups and how well certain products sell.
>
> The disposable income of young people in the UK between the ages of fifteen and twenty-four peaked in 2004 and reached another high point in 2007 before falling sharply. Sales of products typically enjoyed by young people, trainers and video games, showed a similar pattern with sales of both products increasing sharply by 2004 (5% and 6% respectively).
>
> The disposable income of the 35–44 age group peaked in 2008 after reaching its second highest point in 2004. Sales of business suits, books and children's toys – all items that people of this age group might be expected to buy – also peaked in the third quarter of the decade, with particularly strong growth in sales of toys (8%).
>
> For people aged 65–74, disposable income remained roughly constant. Not surprisingly, sales of reading glasses also remained steady throughout the period.
>
> Overall, the figures show that the sales performance of different types of products may be influenced by the disposable income available to different sectors of the population.

1   Look at the three sentences of the introduction. What information is given in each of them?

2   What type of relationship between the two figures is identified and how is this expressed?

3   How is each of the three body paragraphs structured?

4   What specific information has the writer chosen to highlight? Why?

5   What expressions has the writer used to highlight the similarities in the trends represented?

6   What expression is used in the conclusion to express the relationship between the two figures?

> **Exam tip:** If you are presented with two figures which appear to show a cause and effect relationship, it is helpful to take note of this. It will enable you to highlight the information more effectively. However, you should be cautious about expressing a cause and effect relationship too directly. This is because IELTS Writing Task 1 does not ask you to interpret the table or refer to anything outside of it. If you use a cause and effect expression (e.g. *causes*, *leads* to), use a hedging expression to make the claim less sweeping, (e.g. *appears to cause*, *may lead to*), or use one of the expressions in Exercise 3.

3   Look at the two figures below. The two italicized expressions in sentences 1–2 can be used to describe relationships between data sets. Indicate what each of them means by rephrasing the sentence.

1   The two figures show that there is a *positive correlation* between the availability of cheap credit and levels of consumer spending.

2   The two figures show that the rate of taxation *correlates negatively* with levels of consumer spending.

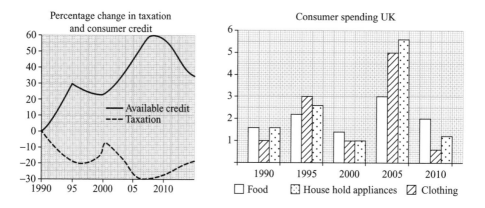

Now rephrase each sentence in three different ways using the expressions a–f below.

a   inversely proportional

b   proportional

c   when ... rises, ... also appear to ...

d   when ... falls, ... appear to ...

e   the less ... the more ...

f   the more ... the more ...

4   Write a description of the two figures in Exercise 3 using the following prompts.

Introduction:
- State what figure 1 shows.
- State what figure 2 shows.

Body paragraph 1:
- Describe the overall relationship between the availability of credit and consumer spending using one of the phrases from Exercise 3.
- Give a more detailed description of the trends.

Body paragraph 2:
- Describe the overall relationship between taxation and consumer spending using one of the phrases from Exercise 3.
- Give a more detailed description of the trends.

Conclusion:
- Rephrase the relationship between credit, taxation and spending.

Part 2:   Practice exercises: Task 2

5   Study the Writing Task 2 question below. Compare the two responses and answer the questions 1–5.

> *What influences our purchasing decisions? Do we mainly buy things because we need them, or are other factors involved?*

Response 1

Sometimes people are more likely to buy products because celebrities have been employed to advertise them. The famous people used in these advertisements make these products more attractive, so people want to purchase them. Therefore, the influence of celebrities can be a powerful reason for some purchasing decisions.

Response 2

Sometimes people are more likely to buy products because celebrities have been employed to advertise them. In buying the product, the consumer may feel 'closer' to a person they admire. An example of this is when famous sportsmen or women endorse a particular brand of trainer or sportswear. Indeed, the powerful influence of this type of advertising on consumer behaviour is reflected in the large sums of money such celebrities are often paid for their advertising work.

1   Which response do you think is more satisfactory? Why?

2   What is the purpose of the first sentence in Responses 1 and 2?

3   What is the purpose of each of the remaining sentences in Response 2?

4   What expression is used to signal that the writer is giving an example?

5   What expression is used to signal that the writer is supporting the main point with evidence?

> **Exam tip:** You can use a range of expressions to signal to the reader that you are giving an example to illustrate your point:
> - *Famous sportsmen and women, **for example/for instance**, may endorse a particular brand of trainer or sportswear.*
> - ***An example/Another good example** of this is when famous sportsmen and women endorse a particular brand of trainer or sportswear.*
>
> And to signal that you are supporting your point with evidence:
> - ***Indeed/In fact** the powerful influence of this type of advertising on consumer behaviour is reflected in the large sums of money such celebrities are often paid for their advertising work.*
>
> The experienced academic reader will normally assume that successive sentences in a passage support or illustrate the points made. For this reason, it is not necessary to use many of these particular signpost expressions to make your passage clear. Two or three in your response will be sufficient in most cases.

6 Complete the text below with signpost expressions.

It is often the case that consumers buy products on impulse simply because of the way they are displayed. In supermarkets, (1) _____, snacks are often situated by the checkout to tempt those who are tired and bored with queuing. (2) _____ is when necessities such as clothes are displayed with matching accessories, such as jewellery. (3) _____ shoppers are often surprised at how much more they spend than they had intended.

7 When thinking about developing a body paragraph, it is useful to ask yourself the following questions:

a What main point do I want to make?

b Have I seen, heard, or experienced something that makes me want to say this? How can I express this as an example to illustrate my main point?

c If someone were to disagree with me, what could I say to persuade them that my point is valid? What evidence can I give to support my main point?

Develop each statement 1–3 below into a paragraph by giving examples and supporting evidence:

1 Some people buy products that they do not really need because they feel empty and unhappy.

2 People often buy products they do not really need because they want to display their status or wealth.

3 Sometimes people buy products they do not really need because they want to use them in a positive way to make their lives more enjoyable or interesting.

8 Look at the IELTS Writing Task 2 question below and write a body paragraph explaining how financial institutions may be responsible for high levels of indebtedness. Remember to make a main point and to give examples to illustrate and support your idea.

> *The increased availability of consumer credit in some countries has contributed to the problem of debt. Who is responsible for high levels of indebtedness: the financial institutions that lend money or the individuals who borrow money?*

Part 3: Exam practice

WRITING TASK 1

You should spend about 20 minutes on this task.

The figures give information about economic growth and household expenditure across a range of categories.

Summarise the information by selecting and reporting the main features, and make comparisons where relevant.

Write at least 150 words.

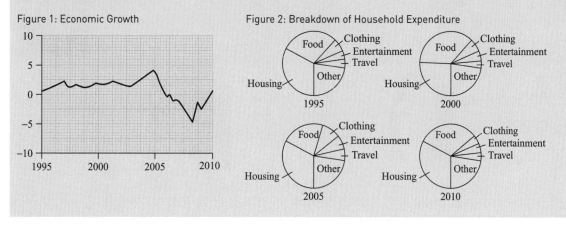

Figure 1: Economic Growth

Figure 2: Breakdown of Household Expenditure

WRITING TASK 2

You should spend about 40 minutes on this task.

Write about the following topic:

Learning to manage money is one of the key aspects of adult life. How in your view can individuals best learn to manage their money?

Give reasons for your answer and include any relevant examples from your own knowledge or experience.

Write at least 250 words.

8 Children and parents

Part 1: Vocabulary

1 Match the words a–e with the words i–v, then indicate which pair of words goes with each of the pictures 1–5 above.

a adult	i old age
b adolescent	ii childhood
c infant	iii adolescence
d pensioner	iv adulthood
e child	v infancy

All of the words listed above are nouns. What is the difference between those in the column on the left and those in the column on the right?

2 The expressions a–j can be associated with rights or responsibilities. Decide which of them are rights and which are responsibilities.

a be entitled to

b have a duty to

c be obliged to

d be empowered to

e be committed to

f be allowed to

g be authorized to

h be permitted to

i be required to

j be held accountable for

3 Underline the verb in each of the sentences 1–5 which expresses the right or responsibility more emphatically.

1 The children were *forced/obliged* to sit still throughout the lesson.

2 Adolescents generally appreciate being *allowed/empowered* to make their own decisions.

3 In some companies, once employees reach the age of sixty-five, they are *compelled/required* to retire.

4 Parents are *committed to doing/have a duty to do* their best for their children.

5 The young men were *required to join/coerced into joining* the army.

4 The sentences 1–8 all contain common set expressions requiring one or more prepositions. Complete the sentences using the prepositions a–h below.

a for   **b** from   **c** in   **d** into   **e** of   **f** on   **g** over   **h** with

1 Parents sometimes want to exercise too much control _____ their children.

2 Young people often perceive their parents as interfering too much _____ their lives.

3 It is often better to negotiate responsibilities _____ adolescents than to impose responsibilities _____ them.

4 Children must learn to cooperate _____ others in order to achieve goals.

5 In some countries such as Scotland, the age _____ criminal responsibility is as low as ten.

6 When setting standards _____ behaviour, the child's level of maturity needs to be taken _____ account.

7 In order for children to distinguish right _____ wrong, they need to be held accountable _____ their actions.

8 Parents do not always behave _____ the best interests _____ their children.

5 Complete the sentences 1–5 below with expressions from Exercise 4.

1 It is unethical if professionals do not act _____ their clients.

2 If a child has a disability, this has to be _____ when deciding on a programme of education.

3 If you are applying for a job which requires teamwork, you need to demonstrate that you are able to _____.

4 When governments impose too many rules and regulations, people often complain that the state is _____.

5 If managers _____ their employees, workers may never develop the ability to take initiative.

Part 2: Practice exercises: Task 1

1 Study the table below, which shows the results of a survey of 200 adolescents and their parents. Compare the two responses and answer questions 1–4.

1 Which response do you think is more satisfactory? Why?

2 Why do you think the writer of Response 2 has chosen to include certain supporting details and not others?

3 How are supporting details in Response 2 signposted and linked with the rest of the text?

4 Are any supporting details supplied without being explicitly signposted?

Parents and Adolescents' Views of Parental Restrictions on Adolescent Decision-Making

Parents should place restrictions on:	Fathers	Mothers	Adolescent girls	Adolescent boys
how adolescents spend their free time	72%	67%	23%	19%
what subject(s) they study	68%	60%	33%	45%
how they spend money they have earned	34%	23%	12%	9%
what occupation they pursue	55%	53%	18%	21%
what friends they make	76%	78%	17%	19%

Response 1

The table shows the results of a survey of 200 adolescents and their parents in which they were asked whether parents should exercise some control over a range of adolescent life choices.

Overall, parents said that they wanted more control over their children than did the adolescents surveyed. For some decisions, the difference in opinion was quite large. In addition, fathers reported wanting more control than mothers over all except one of the choices. Boys were also prepared to accept more parental control than girls in four of the six choices.

Response 2

The table shows the results of a survey of 200 adolescents and their parents in which they were asked whether parents should exercise some control over a range of adolescent life choices.

Overall, parents said that they wanted significantly more control over their children than did the adolescents surveyed. The areas where parents wanted most control were 'how adolescents spend their free time' and 'what friends they make'. Roughly three out of four parents wanted to place restrictions on these areas, whereas only approximately one in five children felt this was needed. The biggest conflict of opinion concerned young people's choice of friends, with nearly 80 per cent of mothers believing they should exercise control and only 17 per cent of adolescent girls agreeing.

In addition, ...

2 Expressions that are commonly used to signal supporting detail include:

- **superlatives:** *most control; the biggest conflict of opinion*
- **focusing expressions:** *particularly, in particular, especially*
- **expressions indicating uniqueness:** *only, sole*
- **expressions indicating example:** *for example, for instance.*

Words used to link supporting detail to main clause include:

- **prepositions:** *with*
- **relative pronouns:** *where, in which*

Look again at the body paragraph in Response 2 on page 66 and at extracts 1–3 below, which are from sample Task 1 responses from previous units. Underline examples of the features listed above.

1 Women predominated in schools for children. This was particularly true of schools for very young children. Over 95 per cent of nursery school teachers, for example, were female. The situation was similarly one-sided in primary schools, where over 90 per cent of teachers were women.

2 In Arts and Social Science-related subjects, UK students tended to do better. The biggest gap in performance was in International Law, where three-quarters of UK students gained a second-class degree or better. In contrast, fewer than half of the international students attained this level.

3 There are four types of writing system in which characters represent sounds. The oldest of these is 'Abjad', in which each character represents a consonant sound. Arabic, for instance, uses this type of system.

3 **Complete the paragraph below with expressions from Exercise 2. For some gaps, there may be more than one correct answer.**

Fathers generally reported wanting more control than mothers, the (1) _____ exception being control over what friends their children make, (2) _____ 76 per cent of fathers, as opposed to 78 per cent of mothers, wanted a say. In addition to choice of friends, fathers were (3) _____ keen to exercise control over how adolescents spend their free time and what they studied. The (4) _____ gap between fathers' and mothers' views was over how children spend their self-earned money. Over a third of fathers wanted to place restrictions on this area, whereas (5) _____ 23 per cent of mothers wanted to do so.

4 **Choose supporting detail from the table in Exercise 1 to complete the paragraph below.**

The adolescent boys surveyed also indicated a greater acceptance of parental control than did the adolescent girls ...

Part 2: Practice exercises: Task 2

5 In order to frame your ideas effectively, you need to use the correct verb forms. You have to choose the correct tense, the correct voice (active or passive) and, where appropriate, the right modal verb. Study the example Task 2 response below to the question: *What can society do to ensure that the rights of young people are respected?* Match the verb forms 1–9 in the text with the functions a–h below. Then answer questions 1–4.

a verb form used when making a promise or prediction _____

b conditional verb form used for describing the consequence(s) of an action _____

c passive voice, often used to describe an action when the agent is unknown or indeterminate _____

d modal verb used to indicate strong obligation or necessity _____

e verb tense indicating that the state or action is habitual, general or true now _____

f modal verb used for making a suggestion and indicating that an action is possible _____

g verb tense used for actions that occurred or were completed in the past _____

h verb tense linking past and present used to express an experience or an ongoing situation _____

i modal verb used for tentatively making a suggestion and indicating possibility _____

In most countries around the world, children (1) *are recognised* as persons by law. However, because children (2) *do not have* the same access to power as adults, they lack the means to defend their rights. It is therefore important that adults recognise the rights of young people. Some argue that this is uniquely the duty of parents. In my view, society as a whole (3) *must* bear some of this responsibility. In this essay I (4) *will outline* three measures that can be taken to safeguard the rights of young people.

Firstly, government (5) *can* ensure that its policies take the interests of children into account. It (6) *could*, for example, appoint a children's commissioner to scrutinise new legislation for compliance with frameworks such as the UN Convention on the Rights of the Child. This (7) *would ensure* that young people are continuously represented in the halls of power.

Secondly, local government and charities can ensure that young people have access to independent confidential sources of help. Telephone help lines are just one example of what could be done. One such service in the UK, Childline, (8) *answered* over 700,000 calls last year, suggesting a strong need for this kind of help.

A third possible measure is to ensure that information about children's rights is widely disseminated through schools, for example, and the mass media. Children who are well-informed about their rights are in a better position to seek help to defend them.

In short, society has an obligation to look after young people. Doing so can have benefits for all. Young people who (9) *have felt* valued by society are more likely to recognise the value of society and behave accordingly.

1 Which verb tense is used most frequently in the text?

2 How many examples of the passive voice are in the response?

3 Which modal verb is used most frequently? Why?

4 Why would you use the modal verb *should* instead of *must*, and why would you use *may*?

Exam tip: Make good use of modal verbs to frame your ideas. Use:
- **will to state your intention:** *In this essay I* **will** *outline three measures that can be taken to safeguard the rights of children.*
- **emphatic modal verbs such as *must* and *should* to express a necessity:** *In my view, society as a whole* **must** *bear some of this responsibility.*
- **can and could to make suggestions:** *Firstly, the government* **can** *ensure that its policies take the interests of children into account.*
- **would to indicate the consequences of implementing a suggestion:** *This* **would** *ensure that young people are continuously represented in the halls of power.*

6 Read the partially completed Task 2 response to the question: *What can be done to encourage young people to become responsible members of society?* Complete the text by adding a modal verb to the gaps 1–10. In some cases more than one modal verb is possible – your choice will depend on how emphatic you wish to be.

In many societies these days, people are concerned about deteriorating standards of behaviour among young people. Petty crime, misuse of drugs and alcohol and apparent lack of respect for others all seem to be on the rise. Some people maintain that the best way to address this problem is to reinstate firm discipline within homes and schools. I (1) _____ suggest that although this (2) _____ be one solution, we (3) _____ approach the task of encouraging responsible behaviour among young people in a variety of ways.

One measure that both parents and teachers (4) _____ take is to involve young people in making decisions about what is acceptable behaviour. In schools for example, teachers (5) _____ draw up a contract with the children in their class. It (6) _____ need to be revised periodically as the children mature and are able to handle more freedom responsibly. Doing this (7) _____ discourage children from using misbehaviour as a means of expressing their independence.

Secondly, young people (8) _____ be taught leadership skills by taking part in organisations such as the Scouts. Young people who have experienced what it is like to be a leader (9) _____ probably have a better understanding of the difficulties involved. This (10) _____ encourage them to cooperate more easily with authority figures ...

Exam tip: Make sure you complete your essay by writing a conclusion, even if this consists of only one sentence. If you are running short of time, it is better to shorten or omit one of your body paragraphs than to fail to complete the task.

7 In conclusions to academic essays, writers often:
a restate their opinion
b summarise the main points
c make a recommendation
d make a prediction (often stating what may happen if the recommended action is or is not taken)

Look at the three conclusions below and notice how the functions a–d have been used.

a The writer gives her opinion.

A more effective approach is to educate the public about the benefits of biodiversity. Money should be invested in the research and development of the world's biological resources. Once people understand that there are real benefits to exploiting natural resources in a sustainable way, they are more likely to make the short-term sacrifices necessary to preserve natural habitats.

d The writer makes a prediction.

b Here the writer summarises the main points.

In brief, it is not possible to make recommendations regarding the supervision of adolescents that fit all contexts. The physical environment, the cultural context, and the personalities of those involved should all be considered.

In short, there is little about today's celebrity culture that is fundamentally more harmful than the types of celebrity children have encountered in the past. Provided children are given appropriate guidance, they are unlikely to be adversely affected.

c The writer makes a recommendation.

Re-read the conclusion to the response in Exercise 5 reproduced below, then answer questions 1–5.

In short, society has an obligation to look after young people. Doing so can have benefits for all. Young people who have felt valued by society are more likely to recognise the value of society and behave accordingly.

1 What expression is used to signal that this is the conclusion?

2 What other expressions can be used for this purpose?

3 Which of the functions a–d above is evident in the first sentence?

4 Which of the functions a–d above is evident in the second sentence?

5 How would you summarise the main points of the essay in a single sentence?

8   Complete the essay in Exercise 6 on page 69 by writing a conclusion. Write one sentence for each of the functions a–d listed in Exercise 7.

Part 3: Exam practice

WRITING TASK 1

You should spend about 20 minutes on this task.

> *The figure shows the results of a survey of 1000 adolescents in five different countries. The participants were asked at what age they believed certain rights and responsibilities should be granted to young people.*
>
> *Summarise the information by selecting and reporting the main features.*

Write at least 150 words.

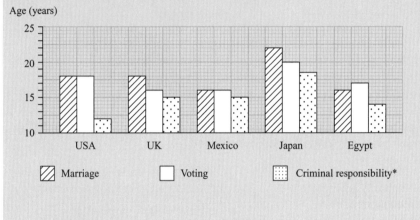

* age at which person who commits a crime can be tried in a court of law

WRITING TASK 2

You should spend about 40 minutes on this task.

Write about the following topic:

> *In many countries, young people are granted certain privileges and responsibilities at the age of sixteen. Clearly parents have a responsibility to both care for and prepare their children as they approach this important milestone.*
>
> *To what degree should parents intervene in the lives of their 14–15 year-old children?*

Give reasons for your answer and include any relevant examples from your own knowledge or experience.

Write at least 250 words.

9 An ageing population

Part 1: Vocabulary

1 The sentences 1–7 all contain words relating to population and population growth. Circle the option (a or b) that the words in italics best correspond to.

1 Overpopulation relates not just to the size of the population but also to the *density* of population in relation to available resources.

    a the total number of people
    b the degree to which an area is filled with people

2 Many people predict that population growth will *accelerate* over the next thirty years before leveling off at approximately 12 billion.

    a stay the same
    b speed up

3 Governments regularly gather *demographic* data, including information about age, gender, income, and employment status, in order to plan effectively for the future.

    a relating to population
    b relating to politics

4 The 2001 *census* revealed that the median age of the population had risen markedly.

    a estimate of the population
    b count of the population

5 The proportion of the population composed of children has declined, while the proportion of the population that is *aged* has grown.

    a old
    b young

6 The recent jump in the numbers of people aged 60 to 65 in some countries can be attributed to the *boom* in births following the Second World War.

    a gradual rise
    b rapid rise

7 As the population ages, many fear that caring for the elderly will be too great a *burden* for the younger generation.

    a obligation
    b privilege

2 Match the expressions 1–10 with the definitions a–j.

1	pension	a	a person who looks after the elderly or sick
2	longevity	b	the ability to produce children
3	nursing home	c	the middle point in a range of values
4	care-giver	d	serious, recurring and/or long lasting
5	to retire	e	long life
6	mortality	f	a regular payment made by government or former employer to a person who has stopped working
7	fertility	g	the control of the number of children in a family by use of contraceptives
8	median	h	to give up work, especially on reaching pensionable age
9	family planning	i	a hospital or home for people who are old or ill
10	chronic	j	the number of deaths in a given period

3 The expressions a–h are either causes or consequences of population ageing. Decide which of them are causes and which are consequences.

a increasing public health costs
b lower fertility rate
c decreasing mortality from infectious diseases
d increasing incidence of chronic illnesses (e.g. arthritis)
e growing pressure on care givers
f family planning
g dwindling pension funds
h improved health care

4 Complete the sentences 1–7 with expressions from Exercise 3. Make any changes necessary.

1 The increasing numbers of older people has put _____, especially women in their 40s, who are also often responsible for looking after children.

2 _____ have been a cause for concern among governments, employers and financial institutions and led to calls for the working population to save more for retirement.

3 _____ has resulted not only in greater longevity but also in better health status among the elderly.

4 _____ such as cholera and polio has been a welcome development.

5 As the population ages, there has been an _____ and type-two diabetes.

6 Unless measures are taken to curb _____, these will almost certainly result in higher taxes.

7 _____ measures have undoubtedly reduced birth rates in some countries.

Part 2:   Practice exercises: Task 1

1   In IELTS Writing Tasks, you need to write coherently, that is link points **within** a sentence and **between** sentences. Study the three short sentences a–c and the longer sentence which combines them. Notice the cohesive devices in italics.

a   Something can be seen from the diagram.

b   Population ageing results from decreasing birth rates.

c   Population ageing results from declining mortality.

As can be seen from the diagram, population ageing results from *both* decreasing birth rates *and* declining mortality.

Cohesive devices include:

pronouns	a Many people enjoy retirement. b Many people find they have the time for activities they enjoy.	Many people enjoy retirement. *They* find they have the time for activities they enjoy.
apposition	a Over the last two decades, population ageing has accelerated in the UK. b Population ageing is a common trend throughout the developed world.	Over the last two decades, population ageing, a common trend throughout the developed world, has accelerated in the UK.
***this/these* + summary word**	a The population in urban areas has grown particularly quickly. b The population growth in urban areas has put pressure on local services.	The population in urban areas has grown particularly quickly. *This trend* has put pressure on local services.
coordinating conjunctions	a There are more job opportunities in cities. b People migrate to cities from rural areas.	There are more job opportunities in cities, *so* people migrate to them from rural areas.
subordinating conjunctions	a Couples are under pressure to work. b Couples often delay starting a family.	*Because* couples are under pressure to work, they often delay starting a family.
relative pronouns	a Lower mortality is due to increased longevity. b Increased longevity results from improved health care.	Lower mortality is due to increased longevity, which results from improved health care.
sentence linkers	a People want to enjoy retirement. b People do not always save enough for a comfortable retirement.	People want to enjoy retirement; *however*, they do not always save enough for a comfortable retirement.

Read the remainder of the paragraph below and underline the cohesive devices.

Decreasing birth rates can be attributed to two main factors, namely: availability of family planning and changes in how people feel about work and family. These changes include greater career aspirations among women, a tendency to delay marriage, and a preference for smaller families. Lower mortality, on the other hand, is due to increased longevity, which results from improved health care and better living conditions.

2 Good cohesion requires a good grasp of punctuation. Look again at the paragraph on page 74 and the longer sentences in the table in Exercise 1. Circle the punctuation marks. Then correct the text below by adding or changing the punctuation.

The graph illustrates two trends. Namely the rise in the proportion of the world's population aged sixty-five and above and the decline in the proportion of those under five. As can be seen the proportion of elderly people has risen gradually from approximately 5 per cent in 1950 to roughly 7.5 per cent today. Over the next thirty years it is expected to more than double. The proportion of young children on the other hand has fallen gradually since 1970 from approximately 14 per cent to 9 per cent, it is forecast to continue falling at roughly the same rate over the next forty years.

3 Combine each group of sentences 1–4 below into one sentence using a range of cohesive devices. Make any changes necessary and punctuate each sentence correctly.

1 The bar chart shows the percentage of people who were over the age of sixty-five in 2000. The bar chart shows the percentage of people expected to be over the age of sixty-five in 2030.The bar chart gives figures for seven different countries.

2 Korea, Mexico, and Turkey are all developing or newly industrialized countries. Korea, Mexico, and Turkey are all expected to experience large increases in the proportion of the population that is elderly.

3 The biggest increase is likely to occur in Korea. The proportion of pensioners in Korea is expected to increase from 10 per cent to 35 per cent.

4 The changes in all three countries will occur from a relatively low base. The predicted proportion of elderly residents will still be lower than that expected in developed economies.

4 Using too many cohesive devices results in writing that is heavy and difficult to read. Improve the paragraph below by removing unnecessary cohesive devices, dividing sentences that are too complex, and correcting the punctuation.

The figure shows the distribution of the population in terms of gender and age, and in fact, the age group with the highest percentage of both men and women is 55 to 59. Moreover, roughly five per cent of the population is in this age group. In addition, the age groups with the next highest proportion of the population are 30 to 34 and 35 to 39. Also, it is interesting that until the age of fifty-nine, the proportion of males and females is roughly equal, however, thereafter, women make up a higher proportion of the elderly population and this trend is particularly evident in those aged eighty. For example, over four per cent of women fall into in this category, whereas only two per cent of men have reached this age.

> **Exam tip:** Remember that readers will assume that each sentence in a paragraph logically develops or supports the preceding sentence unless they are told otherwise. This means that sentence connectors such as *in addition* and *moreover* should be used sparingly, if at all. On the other hand, logical relationships that are surprising or indicate a contrast of ideas normally require signposting expressions such as *however*.

Part 2: Practice exercises: Task 2

5 One of the best ways of achieving good cohesion is through word choice. Read the passage below and answer the questions 1–5.

As the population ages, people can expect to spend a longer proportion of their lives as pensioners. The quality of life among older people has, therefore, become a focus of attention. A number of measures can be taken to ensure that the elderly can enjoy life after retirement.

One of the most important measures is to make sure people of working age are setting aside enough funds for when they retire. This could be done through a government scheme such as the national insurance system in the UK, through employer contributions, or through compulsory private pension plans. Saving sufficient sums of money would ensure that the burden of looking after elderly people does not fall entirely to the younger generation. However, savings alone would probably be insufficient to guarantee a good retirement for all.

Another measure that should be taken is to invest properly in the health care services so that they are able to cope with the demands of an increasingly frail section of the population ...

1 Which sentence captures the main idea of the text?

2 Which key word has the writer repeated in order to make the organisation of the passage clear?

3 In which sentences does this repetition occur?

4 What words and expressions has the writer used to avoid repeating the word *pensioners*?

5 What words and expressions has the writer used to avoid repeating the word *funds*?

> **Exam tip:** Use repetition of key words strategically. It can be effective to repeat two or three times words that link back to the main argument and that make the structure of your response clear. Use synonyms for other words or expressions that you may need to repeat throughout your text.

6 Look at the Task 2 question below and the sample response extract. Notice how the key word *obligations* has been repeated.

1 Write synonyms for the expressions *younger family members* and *older relations* in the blank spaces in the response on page 77.

> *What are the obligations of younger family members towards older relations?*

In most societies, adults in their prime are expected to care for those who are becoming more frail due to old age. How one defines the specific responsibilities of younger family members towards older relations, however, depends on a number of factors, for example, the family's resources and the degree of state support available. Nevertheless, I would suggest a number of core obligations can be identified.

The most fundamental obligation that (younger family members) _____ have towards (older relations) _____ is to ensure that their physical needs are being met. It is particularly important that (older relations) _____ have good nutrition, adequate healthcare and a safe and warm environment. Whether this is provided in the family home or in an institution such as a nursing home does not matter.

Another core obligation is to ensure that (older relations) _____ continue to feel a sense of love and belonging. Whenever possible, they should be included in family occasions such as birthdays, weddings and funerals. Their value to the family as a whole should be acknowledged even if they are no longer able to contribute actively to the family, financially or otherwise.

Finally, (younger family members) _____ should ensure that (older relations) _____ continue to have the opportunity to grow and develop as individuals. As the process of personal development is never complete, people continue to need stimulation in the form of activities and interests throughout their lives. Reading aloud, watching a film together or playing a board game are all things that (younger family members) _____ can do with their (older relations) _____.

In short, ...

Now look at the Task 2 questions below. For each question, circle a key word that you might want to repeat and underline any words or expressions which could be replaced with synonyms.

2   With improvements in life expectancy, people living today are clearly able work productively for much longer than in the past. What are the arguments for and against a mandatory retirement age?

3   What are the most significant consequences of population ageing?

> **Exam tip:** One of the most useful strategies for linking points between sentences is to use the demonstrative *this* or *these*. *This* (or *these*) can be used either on its own or followed by a summary word which captures the main point of the preceding sentence. Study the example below.
>
> *In the past, many* people *believed that people over the age of sixty-five were too old to work.* **This view** *is no longer widely held.*

7 Look at the essay extracts below from sample responses you have seen in previous units. Link the sentences by filling in the gaps with appropriate summary words.

1 The changes that result from allowing men into female-dominated occupations and vice versa may be subtle, but they are far-reaching. However, to benefit the most from this _____, it is important not to expect males and females to approach work in identical ways.

2 However, exams also have clear drawbacks. Test-wise candidates can often perform well in exams without having good underlying knowledge or skills. On the other hand, some test-takers perform poorly in exams simply because of anxiety. Some teachers and learners focus only on those aspects of the curriculum that are likely to be tested, thus narrowing the educational experience for all. A number of measures should be taken to address these _____.

3 Governments could promote greater understanding of plants and animals by investing in the research and preservation efforts of universities, zoos and botanical institutes... However, this _____ alone would do little to protect whole ecosystems that are under threat.

4 It is true that as the balance of power among groups of people throughout history has shifted, languages have arisen, changed, and died out. Even once widely spoken languages, such as Latin, have disappeared. To some extent, therefore, this _____ may be inevitable.

8 Study the topic sentences which open the three body paragraphs of the response in Exercise 6 (reproduced below). Underline the word or phrase in each that signals it is a topic sentence. Circle the phrase that that expresses the main idea developed in the paragraph.

1 The most fundamental obligation that younger family members have towards older relations is to ensure that their physical needs are being met.

2 Another core obligation is to ensure that older relations continue to feel a sense of love and belonging.

3 Finally, younger family members should ensure that older relations continue to have the opportunity to grow and develop as individuals.

Now write topic sentences for three paragraphs in response to the question below.

> *What are the most significant consequences of population ageing?*

Use repetition and synonyms as appropriate.

Expand the first topic sentence into a paragraph. Make your paragraph cohesive using *this* (or *these*) + a summary word.

Part 3:   Exam practice

WRITING TASK 1

You should spend about 20 minutes on this task.

> *The figure shows demographic trends in Scotland.*
>
> *Summarise the information by selecting and reporting the main features.*

Write at least 150 words.

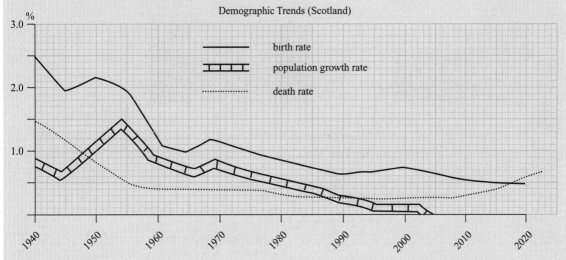

WRITING TASK 2

You should spend about 40 minutes on this task.

Write about the following topic:

> *Longer life spans and improvements in the health of older people suggest that people over the age of sixty-five can continue to live full and active lives.*
>
> *In what ways can society benefit from the contribution that older people can make?*

Give reasons for your answer and include any relevant examples from your own knowledge or experience.

Write at least 250 words.

10 Fame

Part 1: Vocabulary

1 In IELTS Writing Tasks, it is important to demonstrate that you have a wide vocabulary by avoiding unnecessary repetition. Match the words 1–9 with the words a–i that have a similar meaning.

1	fame	a	short-lived
2	ambition	b	icon
3	achievement	c	accomplishment
4	shortcoming	d	approve
5	idol	e	stardom
6	transient	f	aspiration
7	endorse	g	notorious
8	image	h	flaw
9	infamous	i	impression

2 Knowing which words go together is important. Complete the sentences 1–6 with words from Exercise 1 above to form common collocations. Make any necessary changes to part of speech or number.

1 When meeting someone for the first time, it is natural to want to make a good _____.

2 When starting a new project, it is common to be full of hopes and _____.

3 Many people see celebrities as being all _____ and no substance.

4 People often migrate to cities seeking _____ and fortune.

5 Although he is undoubtedly famous, his character is deeply _____.

6 She aspired to being a fashion _____.

3 Sometimes an idea can be expressed with greater or lesser degrees of strength by a group of words or phrases with similar meanings. For example: *satisfactory good excellent.* Arrange the groups of words below from left to right in terms of strength of meaning.

1 famous   legendary   well-known
2 bad   imperfect   worthless
3 like   admire   idolise
4 praise   acclaim   recognition

4 The adverbs below can be placed at the beginning of a statement to show your attitude to what follows. Rewrite the sentences 1–7, beginning each sentence with an adverb that expresses the sentence in brackets.

fortunately   interestingly   surprisingly
importantly   obviously   unfortunately
inevitably

1 Many people who achieve fame as children struggle to live a normal adult life. (This phenomenon is bound to happen.)

_____

2 Many people who become famous as children struggle to live a normal life in adulthood. (This is not a good thing.)

_____

3 Only a small percentage of people become truly obsessed with celebrities. (This is a good thing.)

_____

4 The vast majority of respondents were critical of the amount of celebrity coverage in the news. (I didn't expect this.)

_____

5 Fame can confer certain advantages. (This is clear.)

_____

6 The majority of children surveyed said that they did not want to be famous. (I find this interesting.)

_____

7 Many children were critical of the bad behaviour of people in the public eye. (This idea is significant.)

_____

5 Some of the adverbs above can be modified by the use of: *more, less, not, somewhat.* Complete the sentences 1–4 below with an adverb and suitable modifier.

1 Fame can be stressful. (This is not as clear as the previous point.)

_____

2 The majority of children said they did not want to emulate the bad behaviour of their idols. (This idea is more significant than the previous one.)

_____

3 People find notorious criminals quite fascinating. (This is to be expected.)

_____

4 The children of famous people rarely seek fame themselves. (This is a bit surprising.)

_____

Part 2: Practice exercises: Task 1

1 Sentences 1–8 describe information in the table below, which compares the results of a survey of children's career aspirations in 1980 and 2010. Each sentence contains two commonly confused words in italics. Underline the correct word.

rank	1980	%	2010	%
1	Teacher	14	Sports star	13
2	Businessman/woman	9	Actor/Actress	12
3	Doctor/Nurse	8	Popular singer	11
4	Scientist	7	Astronaut	9
5	Lawyer	6	Lawyer	8
6	Vet	6	Businessman/woman	8
7	Sports star	5	Doctor/Nurse	6
8	Astronaut	4	Teacher	6
9	Banker	4	Chef	5
10	Archaeologist	3	Vet	4

1 Children today appear to have a greater interest in careers associated with celebrities than did children in the *passed/past*.

2 Surprisingly, the *number/percentage* of children wanting to work in medicine decreased.

3 There were changes in the rankings of all of the occupations *accept/except* that of lawyer.

4 The percentage of children choosing 'sports star' as one of their top ten careers *rose/raised*.

5 In 2010, a higher proportion of children wanted to work in entertainment *then/than* in traditional professions such as medicine.

6 A *smaller/fewer* percentage of respondents opted for 'teacher' in 2010 than in 1980.

7 *In contrast/On the contrary*, a much higher percentage of those surveyed chose 'sports star', which occupies first position in the 2010 list.

8 Some professions that did not appear in the 1980 rankings, *feature/future* prominently in the 2010 list.

Now complete the sentences 9–13 below with some of the words in italics above.

9 The percentage of children wanting to be an astronaut _____.

10 In 2010, a _____ percentage of children wanted to be a vet.

11 A smaller percentage of children today want to work in business and banking than did children in the _____.

12 Not surprisingly, 'banker' did not _____ in the 2010 list.

13 All of the professions in the 1980 list appeared in the 2010 list _____ scientist, astronaut and banker.

2 The paragraph below contains six informal expressions in italics. Replace them with more appropriate words or expressions.

There were (1) *really big* changes in the children's career aspirations between 1980 and 2010. (2) *Lots of* traditional professions either declined in popularity or disappeared. (3) *E.g.* in 1980, 14 per cent of respondents wanted to be teachers whereas thirty years later, only 6 per cent of those surveyed chose this profession. (4) *Amazingly*, scientist, ranked fourth in 1980, (5) *didn't* even (6) *show up* in the top ten occupations of 2010.

1 _____   4 _____

2 _____   5 _____

3 _____   6 _____

3 The passage below contains some unnecessary repetition. Replace the words 1–6 in italics with synonyms from Exercise 1 on page 82. Make any other necessary changes to the words.

A number of professions typically associated with celebrities, which were not included in the 1980 list, appeared among the top ten in 2010. Acting and singing were particularly popular, ranking second and third respectively. Chef, chosen by five per cent of respondents, also (1) *appeared* in the 2010 list. Other (2) *professions* increased significantly in popularity. The percentage of (3) *respondents* (4) *choosing* sports star and astronaut more than doubled. The only (5) *profession* that did not change in the rankings was lawyer, which (6) *appeared in* fifth place in both 1980 and 2010.

1 _____   4 _____

2 _____   5 _____

3 _____   6 _____

4 The words in italics in the extracts 1–7 from unit 2 below are too informal. Rewrite the sentences using more appropriate words and phrases.

1 One of the *biggest steps* in civilisation is the development of modern *ways of making and getting food ready.*

_____

_____

2 Convenience foods have now become the *done thing* in many societies.

_____

_____

3 Although some people *love* traditional cooking practices and believe they will *be around for a long time,* ...

_____

_____

4 In more traditional societies, where families tended to be big, it made economic sense for one person to *give* him/herself to time-consuming *jobs at home* such as growing and preparing food.

_____

_____

5 Nowadays, people *by and large* live in ever smaller family units.

_____

_____

6 If each family were to spend *hours and hours* growing and processing food, this would be a *silly* use of society's human resource.

_____

_____

7 ... the increase in the number of *grown ups*, especially women with *kids*, who work *in jobs all day long*.

_____

_____

5 The table below shows the results of an opinion poll of media coverage. Read the description and circle the most appropriate option in the items 1–7 in italics. Then underline the expressions the writer has used to avoid repeating the word *respondents*.

Too much coverage of:	%	Too little coverage of:	%
Celebrity gossip	42	Good news	18
Political leaders	10	Poverty/Homelessness	11
War/Conflict	9	Environment	10
Crime	8	Education	9
The economy/recession	8	Health	8
Sports	5	International news	4

The table presents the findings of a public opinion survey of media coverage.

On the whole, the respondents felt there was too much coverage of individuals in the entertainment industry and politics, 'bad' news and sports. Dissatisfaction with the amount of coverage given to celebrity gossip was particularly high at 42 per cent. Individuals in politics were also seen as (1) *receiving/getting* too much attention by one in ten of those surveyed. A similar (2) *number/percentage* of respondents said the media focused too much on (3) *awful/negative* news stories, war and the recession, for example. At the other end of the scale, a (4) *small/few* percentage of people questioned said there was too much sports news. (5) *On the contrary/On the other hand*, respondents said that there (6) *wasn't/was not* enough coverage of good news, social and issues and international news. Nearly one in five of those who took part in the survey felt that there was not enough focus on good news. A relatively high percentage also felt that there was too little coverage of issues relating to quality of life: poverty, the environment, education and health. A small percentage (4 per cent) wanted more international news.

In short, (7) *there appears to be/you could say there was* a mismatch between the types of news stories covered and the stated preferences of the survey respondents.

Part 2: Practice exercises: Task 2

6 The language required for IELTS Writing Task 2 is often quite predictable. Listed below are ten common expressions. Write one or two words with a similar meaning for each.

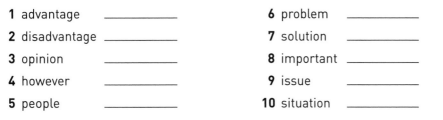

1 advantage   _____   6 problem   _____

2 disadvantage _____   7 solution   _____

3 opinion   _____   8 important _____

4 however   _____   9 issue   _____

5 people   _____   10 situation   _____

7 Study the four introductions a–d to an essay written in response to the question:
In your view, why have celebrities become such an important feature of modern life?
Answer questions 1–2.

1 Which is the best introduction?

2 What is the problem with each of the other three?

    a There are more and more television programmes, magazines, and newspaper articles about celebrities these days. The 'cult of celebrity' is one of the one of the things about modern pop culture that really stands out. Some people say that because there have always been famous people around, this isn't anything new. But I say that there's something different about fame today.

    b The number of television programmes, magazines, and newspaper articles focusing on the lives of celebrities has rocketed over the last few decades. Indeed, the 'cult of celebrity' is the defining feature of modern popular culture. People say that, because there have always been famous people, this is not a new phenomenon. However, I insist that fame today is unique to our times.

    c The number of television programmes, magazines, and newspaper articles focusing on the lives of celebrities appears to have grown considerably over the last few decades. Indeed, the 'cult of celebrity' seems to be one of the defining features of modern popular culture. Some people insist that, because there have always been famous people, this is not a new phenomenon. However, I would suggest that there are aspects of fame today that are particular to our times.

    d The number of television programmes, magazines, and newspaper articles focusing on the lives of celebrities appears to have grown considerably over the last few decades. Indeed, the 'cult of celebrity' seems to be one of the defining features of television programmes, magazines and newspapers. Some people insist that, because there have always been famous people, the 'cult of celebrity' is not a new phenomenon. However, I would suggest that there are aspects of the 'cult of celebrity' that are particular to our times.

8 Read the first two body paragraphs of the essay on page 86. Improve the text by:

1 changing the informal expressions into more formal language. (The first one has been marked for you in italics.)

2 adding hedges to the statements 1–5 that are too sweeping. Use the hints to help you.

Add a hedge to show that this is a generalisation.	In the past, people (1) _____ became famous for *doing great things*. Einstein, Dickens, and Gandhi, for instance, were all celebrated for what they'd done for science, literature and public life. People	
Add a hedge to show that this is not the only reason.	were interested in them (2) _____ because they were role models. One of the reasons fame today is so different is because celebrities (3) _____ meet a	Add a hedge to indicate that this seems to be what happens.
	range of people's emotional needs, not just the need for role models. Lots of people in the public eye today are famous simply for being famous. The public are (4) _____	
Add a hedge that indicates this is a possibility.	interested in them because, when news of scandals comes out into the open, they (5) _____ get the satisfaction of feeling superior to people they've been encouraged to envy.	Add a hedge to indicate that this doesn't happen all of the time.

9 Read the third body paragraph and the conclusion to the essay below. Reduce the unnecessary repetition in the text by replacing repeated words with synonyms.

Another reason fame today is unique is the desire for ordinary people to explore the nature of fame itself. Many celebrities that have emerged from reality television programmes, for example, come from the same walks of life as ordinary people. Reading about or watching such celebrities allow ordinary people to imagine what it might be like to suddenly find themselves in the public eye. Celebrities may, therefore, allow ordinary people to indulge in wish fulfilment fantasies without having to worry about whether they are capable of significant achievement.

The third and perhaps most significant reason that celebrities play such an important role in modern life is the fact that commercial pressures encourage media organisations to focus on information that is immediately attractive to ordinary people. As we have seen, celebrities appear to tap into powerful emotional needs, the need to feel superior, the need to imagine oneself to be the centre of attention; therefore, news about celebrities sells.

> **Exam tip:** Remember that some repetition is acceptable and can even be effective as a means of signposting key ideas. If you do not know suitable synonyms for some key terms, it is better to repeat these words than to use expressions that are a poor match or inappropriate to the context.

10 Read the concluding paragraph below. Make any changes to word choice and style that you think necessary.

In brief, the nature of fame today is different from fame in the past. There's a greater need to denigrate, rather than celebrate the actions of people in the public eye, as well as huge interest in fame itself. Whether the public will eventually get tired of denigrating people in the public eye or of fame itself we'll never know.

Part 3: Exam practice

WRITING TASK 1

You should spend about 20 minutes on this task.

> *The table shows the results of a survey of people's perception of celebrity news coverage.*
>
> *Summarise the information by selecting and reporting the main features, and make comparisons where relevant.*

Write at least 150 words.

Celebrities receive:	%	Who is responsible for the amount of coverage?	%	Who gives celebrities the most coverage?	%
too much news coverage	85	news organisations	56	television news	60
not enough news coverage	6	the public	34	Internet news websites	15
right amount of coverage	7	both	7	newspapers	12
don't know	2	don't know	3	radio news	5
				other	3
				don't know	5

WRITING TASK 2

You should spend about 40 minutes on this task.

Write about the following topic:

> *Many people believe that media coverage of celebrities is having a negative effect on children.*
>
> *To what extent do you agree or disagree with this opinion?*

Give reasons for your answer and include any relevant examples from your own knowledge or experience.

Write at least 250 words.

11 The car

Part 1: Vocabulary

1   **Match the phrases a–h with the road signs 1–8 above.**

a   cycle route ahead

b   frail pedestrians likely ahead

c   end of motorway

d   traffic queues likely

e   road works ahead

f   danger

g   bus lane at road junction ahead

h   speed cameras in the area

2   **Use the words and phrases from Exercise 1 above to complete the sentences 1–7. Make any necessary changes.**

1   Unless the government invests in _____, the number of journeys made by bicycle is unlikely to increase.

2   Although _____ have been shown to reduce the frequency of road accidents, drivers dislike being under surveillance.

3   Faulty traffic lights and inadequate road crossings put the lives of _____ in _____.

4   In spite of the government's expansion of the road network, drivers are still likely to experience _____ during peak travel periods.

5   _____ make travelling long distances much faster; however, many people feel they are a blight on the landscape.

6   The need to continually upgrade and repair the road network means that journeys are frequently delayed by _____.

7   The number of journeys by public transport increased when the government invested in _____ and the commuter rail network.

3   For IELTS Writing, you have to show not only that you have a wide vocabulary but also that you can use the right form of a word in the right context. Complete the table below with the correct word forms.

verb	noun
_____	reduction
_____	production
convert	_____
maintain	_____
_____	emission
combust	_____
propel	_____

4   Use words from Exercise 3 to complete the passage below. Make any changes necessary.

Electric cars are battery-powered vehicles (1) _____ by electric motors. Because electric cars are more efficient at (2) _____ stored energy into (3) _____ they have the potential to (4) _____ CO2 emissions. The level of reduction depends on how the electricity is generated; however, it can be substantial. In the UK, for example, if vehicles with internal (5) _____ engines were replaced with electric vehicles, CO2 (6) _____ would decrease by 40 per cent. Moreover, because electric cars do not (7) _____ exhaust fumes, they have the potential to reduce urban pollution. Another advantage of electric cars is their low (8) _____ costs; because electric motors have fewer moving parts than petrol-powered engines, they are easier to maintain. One disadvantage, however, is that they (9) _____ less noise and can therefore be dangerous to pedestrians.

Governments and manufacturers around the world are investing substantial sums in the development of state-of-the-art electric cars and batteries. Some have predicted that electric car (10) _____ will increase substantially over the next decade and that by 2025, 12 per cent of cars on the road will be battery-powered.

5   Look again at the nouns in Exercise 3 and notice how they all end in: -tion, -sion, or -ance. Another common ending for nouns which are frequently used in academic writing is –ment. Write the noun form of the verbs a–g. Use -tion, -sion, -ance, or -ment and make any other changes necessary to the root form of the word. Then complete the sentences 1–7 with the correct noun form.

a   achieve _____   c   allow _____   e   involve _____   g   oppose _____
b   appear _____   d   explain _____   f   provide _____

1   The local authority was unable to enforce the new parking restrictions because of significant public _____.
2   For many people, learning to dive is a significant _____.
3   The train operator could not offer a coherent _____ for why the trains were frequently late.
4   When purchasing a new car, people will often consider functionality, price and _____.
5   The new public transport scheme is unlikely to go ahead unless there is substantial financial _____ from central government.
6   It is important that drivers make _____ for cyclists on busy roads.
7   Attempts to create pedestrian-only zones in city centres are unlikely to succeed without the _____ of local businesses.

Part 2: Practice exercises: Task 1

1 Many of the most common errors in candidates' Task 1 responses involve tense. Complete the sentences 1–6 by selecting the correct tense a, b, or c.

1 Between 2008 and 2009, there ___ a substantial decrease in petrol prices.
   a was
   b has been
   c is

2 Petrol prices ___ substantially since 2009.
   a rose
   b have risen
   c are rising

3 The figure shows that if the price of petrol ___ to rise over the next five years, fewer people will choose to drive.
   a will continue
   b continues
   c is continuing

4 As a general rule, car use ___ positively with per capita income.
   a correlates
   b is correlating
   c was correlating

5 The percentage of households in the UK with access to a car ___ from 50 per cent to 73 per cent between 1975 and 2000.
   a is increasing
   b was increasing
   c increased

6 According to the graph, car use ___ substantially when the oil crisis began.
   a already rose
   b was already rising
   c will rise

2 Another common difficulty with Task 1 responses is knowing when to use the active voice and when to use the passive voice. Underline the correct form in the sentences 1–6 below.

1 Sales of electric cars *decreased/were decreased* for approximately three years.

2 Over the next ten years, electric car sales *expect/are expected* to rise.

3 Petrol consumption *correlates/is correlated* negatively with population density.

4 Use of public transport *varied/was varied* in relation to income and average distance travelled per year.

5 Public transport *accounted/was accounted* for only eight per cent of journeys to work in 2010.

6 When they *asked/were asked* why they were reluctant to buy an electric car, the majority of respondents cited the following factors: cost, maintenance and reliability.

3 It is important to know when to use the infinitive, the infinitive without *to*, or the *-ing* form of a verb. For each sentence 1–6, write the correct form of the verb in brackets.

1 Three-quarters of the survey participants said that, whenever possible, they avoided _____ (drive) at peak times.

2 People below the age of twenty-five and over the age of fifty-five tended _____ (use) public transport more regularly than those aged between twenty-six and fifty-four.

3 Consumers often postpone _____ (purchase) a new car during periods of economic uncertainty.

4 Even significant discounts on new car models did not make prospective buyers _____ (change) their minds.

5 Nearly half the respondents indicated that they would consider _____ (travel) by public transport if it were cheaper and more reliable.

6 Most people said that they intended _____ (reduce) their car use in future.

Exam tip: One of the most common errors is that of article use. Often it is difficult to correct because the rules of article use in English are complex. Most mistakes can be avoided by following a few basic guidelines:

- make generalisations using the plural noun without *the*: *Cars cause pollution.*
- single countable nouns generally require an article.
  - use *a* if you mean *one* or *any*: *Most people would buy **a** new car if they could afford one.*
  - use *the* if you mean a specific one: ***The** car that I bought last year…*
- use *the* with:
  - ordinals: ***The** first car I ever bought…,*
  - superlatives: ***The** best car on the market…,*
  - words such as *only*, *sole*, or *same*: ***The** only electric car costing less than £20,000…*
  - adjectives to represent a class of people: ***The** wealthy could afford cars.*

4   **Study the Task 1 response below. Complete the text by adding prepositions and articles *a* and *the*. Where no article or preposition is needed write – .**

The bar chart gives information about (1) _____ modes of transport used (2) _____ people living in rural areas and cities of (3) _____ different sizes. It shows the annual distance travelled by car, bus, train and (4) _____ foot per person.

Overall, the distance travelled is inversely proportional (5) _____ the size of conurbation. People living in (6) _____ large cities (over, 50,000 inhabitants) travelled less than those living in cities (7) _____ fewer than 50,000 people and considerably less than those living in rural areas. Inhabitants of (8) _____ largest cities (over 500,000) travelled the fewest miles (approximately 5,500). In contrast, (9) _____ people living in the countryside travelled nearly twice that distance each year.

This tendency was particularly evident in relation (10) _____ car travel. For all of the categories represented, cars considerably outweighed other forms of transport. However, people living in (11) _____ rural area travelled nearly three times the distance (over 9,000 miles) by car as people living in (12) _____ large city. In fact, car use correlated negatively with (13) _____ size of the conurbation.

Other modes of transport, on the other hand, showed (14) _____ opposite tendency. The inhabitants of larger cities tended to travel more by train and bus and on foot than people in less populated areas.

In short, city living appears to be more environmentally friendly, at least as far as distance and mode of transport is concerned.

Exam tip: Make sure that you are familiar with the type of mistakes that you tend to make. Look at previous texts you have written and draw up a list of your four or five most common mistakes. Keep them in mind when you check your work.

Part 2: Practice exercises: Task 2

5   Ten of the most common errors found in Task 2 responses involve problems with a–f below.

a subject-verb agreement
b articles: a/an/the
c countable vs. uncountable nouns
d prepositions
e part of speech

f relative clauses
g verb forms: modal/infinitive/gerund
h tenses
i run-on sentences
j sentence fragments

The sentences 1–10 each contain one of the errors a–j listed above. Identify the type of error in each sentence and correct it.

1 The evidences show that wearing a seatbelt significantly reduces road accident fatalities.

2 In fact wearing a seatbelt is most important safety measure that can be taken.

3 The number of road accidents has declined last year.

4 It is illegally to drive without a licence.

5 The cost of insurance depends of several factors including age, experience and type of car.

6 Organisations such as the AA can to provide assistance to motorists who break down.

7 Many people which living in rural areas have no choice but to travel by car.

8 Buying a second-hand car is sometimes risky, inexperienced buyers can be easily cheated.

9 There is numerous examples of illegal practices in the second-hand motor trade.

10 Because the industry is poorly regulated and buyers are not always well-informed.

6   **Correct use of relative clauses can demonstrate good control of complex sentence structure. Join the pairs of sentences 1–5 using a relative pronoun. N.B. There may be more than one way of joining the sentences. Choose the way that most effectively highlights the main point.**

1   Some people own cars. Cars undoubtedly have practical benefits for them.

_____

2   Urban pollution can lead to respiratory problems such as asthma. Urban pollution is largely caused by vehicle emissions.

_____

3   Cars cause noise pollution. Noise pollution is another problem that can affect people's health.

_____

4   The vast majority of car journeys are for short distances. Short distances can be covered on foot.

_____

5   There is evidence that some people are less likely to know or interact with their neighbours. These people live on streets with high volumes of traffic.

_____

7 Having good control of sentence structure also means having good control of punctuation. Correct the punctuation in the sentences 1–7.

1 Although most people say they would use other forms of transport for short journeys in fact most car journeys are for distances of less than two miles.

2 Most people are reluctant to buy electric cars because of three main factors, cost, maintenance and reliability.

3 Some of those surveyed said they had concerns about the distance electric cars could travel before having to be recharged.

4 Electric cars are more expensive than conventional cars, however their maintenance costs are lower.

5 One major Japanese car manufacturer which produces some of the most fuel-efficient petrol-powered cars has recently announced that it plans to invest more heavily in electric car technology.

6 By 2025 over 40 per cent of vehicles on the road are likely to be hybrid or electric cars.

7 Hybrid and electric cars produce fewer emissions but this may not result in a reduction in overall emissions. Because the growth in car ownership over the next fifteen years is likely to accelerate.

8 For IELTS Writing Task 2, it is important that you give reasons for your opinions. Connect the pairs of sentences 1–5 using the linking words given in brackets.

1 In many parts of the world, people now have greater access to cars. They often have more choice over where they live and work. (as)

_____

_____

2 Cities have become more sprawling. People have sought out the greater privacy and space afforded by suburban living. (because)

_____

_____

3 There are more vehicles, often travelling at greater speed. The streets are less hospitable to pedestrians. (as a consequence)

_____

_____

4 There has also been a decline in public transport. People have less day-to-day contact with other members of their community. (as a result)

_____

_____

5 Most people are very dependent on their cars. Most people do not want to give up their cars. (since)

_____

_____

9   The essay extract below contains three run-on sentences, two very short sentences and one sentence fragment. Repair the text by correcting the punctuation and choosing from the list of linking words below to connect the ideas. (N.B. there are more linking words than needed.)

although	since
as	therefore
as a consequence	whereas
because	which
however	while

In many parts of the world, people now have greater access to cars, they often have more choice over where they live and work. Cities have become more sprawling, people have sought out the greater privacy and space afforded by suburban living. There are more vehicles. Often travelling at greater speed. The streets are less hospitable to pedestrians. There has also been a decline in public transport, people have less day-to-day contact with other members of their community.

> **Exam tip:** It is worthwhile learning how to effectively proofread your writing. Always check your work carefully and correct any mistakes you find.

10   Read the following essay extract written in response to the question: *What are the most significant negative consequences of the massive expansion of car ownership?* Find and correct as many of the errors as you can but don't be disappointed if you don't find all of them.

One of the factor that distinguishes developed from developing economies is mass car ownership. Cars undoubtedly have practical benefits for the individuals which own them. They allow for more flexible and autonomous travel. Like other consumer items, they can be used to expressing individual taste and identity, however, they also clearly have a number of undesirable consequences.

One of these consequences is deteriorate in people's health. Urban pollution which is largely causing by vehicle emissions. It can cause respiratory problems such as asthma. This health problems is more prevalent in cities, particularly among children and the elderly. Noise pollution caused by car is another problem that can affect on people's health.

Another consequences of car use is a decline in levels of physical activity and hence levels of fitness. Although this is partly a consequence of rising prosperity generally, there is evidence that car use is responsible to lower levels of cardiovascular fitness. The vast majority of car journeys are for less than two miles, that is, distances that can easily be covered on foot. In short, when people own the cars, they tend to walk less, thus removing a major means by which people maintain day-to-day fitness.

Finally, widespread car use can have a negative effect on community life. There is evident that people who live on streets with high volumes of traffic are less likely to know or interact with their neighbours. This too can have a negative impact on people's sense of well-being.

These factors alone are unlikely to discourage people from buying cars. However, more could be done to make the public more aware of the disadvantages of car ownership. Provide alternative means of transport would encourage people to use their cars less and enjoy some of the benefits of a car-free environment.

Part 3: Exam practice

WRITING TASK 1

You should spend about 20 minutes on this task.

> *The table shows the percentage of journeys made by different forms of transport in four countries. The bar chart shows the results of a survey into car use.*
>
> *Summarise the information by selecting and reporting the main features, and make comparisons where relevant.*

Write at least 150 words.

Journeys made by:	USA	UK	France	Netherlands
Car	90%	72%	68%	47%
Bicycle	1%	2%	2%	26%
Public transport	3%	12%	18%	8%
On foot	5%	11%	11%	18%
Other	1%	3%	1%	1%

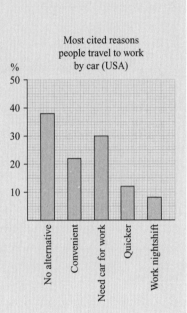

Most cited reasons people travel to work by car (USA)

WRITING TASK 2

You should spend about 40 minutes on this task.

Write about the following topic:

> *There is a good deal of evidence that increasing car use is contributing to global warming and having other undesirable effects on people's health and well-being.*
>
> *What can be done to discourage people from using their cars?*

Give reasons for your answer and include any relevant examples from your own knowledge or experience.

Write at least 250 words.

12 Practice test

WRITING TASK 1

You should spend about 20 minutes on this task.

> *The figure gives information about smoking habits of the UK population by age.*
>
> *Summarise the information by selecting and reporting the main features, and make comparisons where relevant.*

Write at least 150 words.

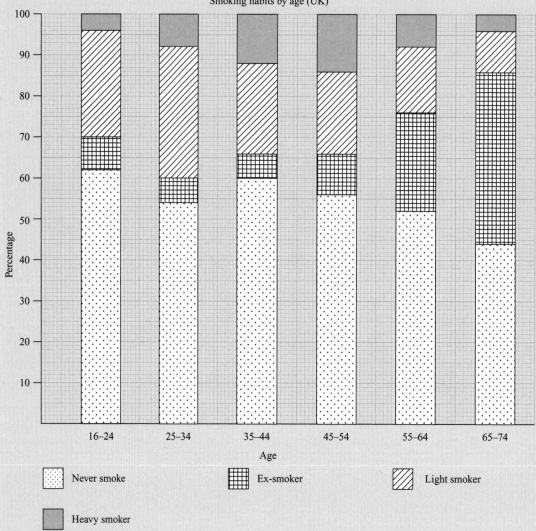

Smoking habits by age (UK)

WRITING TASK 2

You should spend about 40 minutes on this task.

Write about the following topic:

> *In recent years, there has been growing interest in the relationship between inequality and personal achievement. Some people believe that individuals can achieve more in more egalitarian societies. Others believe that high levels of personal achievement are possible only if individuals are free to succeed or fail according to their individual merits.*
>
> *What is your view of the relationship between equality and personal success?*

Give reasons for your answer and include any relevant examples from your own knowledge or experience.

Write at least 250 words.

Additional model essays

Unit 1

Bar charts are frequently used to compare information. Notice how the writer makes comparisons throughout.

The writer makes reference to only four percentage figures out of a possible total of twelve. This is enough to illustrate and support the main points. Remember, you do not need to include all of the information in the visual prompt.

The response meets the 150 word requirement but is not any longer than necessary. Remember, you should spend no more than twenty minutes on Task 1.

Unit 1 – Task 1

The chart compares the percentage of male and female teachers in different educational settings from nursery school to university. Significant differences between men and women are evident.

Women held nearly all of the teaching posts in nursery and primary schools and the majority of posts in secondary schools (approximately 56 per cent). They held the same percentage of posts as did men at college level. However, a smaller proportion of women held teaching positions at training institutes, and, at universities, female lecturers were outnumbered by males by roughly two to one.

For men, the pattern of employment was the reverse. Only 2 per cent of nursery school teachers and 10 per cent of primary teachers were men. They were more equally represented at secondary and college level. However, a significantly higher percentage of university lecturers were male (roughly 70 per cent).

Overall, the figure shows that gender is a significant factor in patterns of employment within the education sector.

(151 words)

The bar chart represents percentages not numbers. The words *percentage* and *proportion* are used throughout the response.

The conclusion highlights the main point but does not offer an explanation. You are not required to explain or interpret the data.

Unit 2

This is a response to a Type D 'Evaluate an idea' essay question. It asks the writer to consider the truth value of a prediction.

The writer structures her essay around reasons for her opinion. Notice how the word *reason* appears at the start of each body paragraph.

The response meets the 250-word requirement.

Unit 2 – Task 2

One of the most significant advances in civilisation is the development of modern methods of food production and preparation. Convenience foods have now become the norm in many societies. Although some people idealise traditional cooking practices and believe they will prevail indefinitely, demographic trends suggest that this is unlikely to be the case. In fact, there are a number of reasons for believing that convenience foods are likely to grow in popularity.

The first reason is the decline in family size and the increase in single-adult households. In more traditional societies, where families tended to be large, it made economic sense for one person to devote him/herself to time-consuming domestic tasks such as growing and preparing food. Nowadays, people tend to live in ever smaller family units. If each family were to spend large amounts of time growing and processing food, this would be a poor use of society's human resource.

Another reason convenience foods are likely to become more popular is the increase in the number of adults, especially women with children, who work in full-time employment. In the UK, for example, working mothers significantly outnumber stay-at-home mothers. There is evidence that consumption of convenience foods rises with numbers of hours worked. As modern life increasingly demands that people are economically active, this trend is likely to continue.

Although many people still value traditional foods and methods of cooking, the trend towards smaller, dual-income households suggests that convenience foods are likely to continue to grow in popularity and may very well eventually replace traditional methods of food production and preparation.

(261 words)

By acknowledging there is another point of view, the writer indicates that she has 'tested' her idea.

Examples to illustrate and support the argument are also given.

Unit 3

Unit 3 – Task 1

The simple present tense is used when referring to what the figure shows.

The bar chart shows the percentage of home and international students in the UK achieving at least a second class degree in eight subjects in 2009.

Quantities are referred to in a variety of ways.

The simple past tense is used here and in the remainder of the response because the data refers to 2009.

For the UK students, over half of the degrees awarded were second class or better. The largest percentage of good passes was in Art History and Sociology (80 per cent) The lowest was in Information Technology (55 per cent).

The writer uses superlatives when comparing more than two items, (in this case, eight subjects).

For international students, the rates were similarly high, though figures for individual subjects differed. In Electrical Engineering and Information Technology, four out of five degrees awarded to students from abroad were second class or better (versus fewer than two out of three for home students). However, the percentage gaining good degrees in subjects such as English Literature (55 per cent) and Law (50 per cent) was lower than the corresponding rate for home students (roughly 70 per cent).

The writer uses comparatives when comparing two items, (in this case, international and home students).

The conclusion highlights the main idea but does not give reasons.

In brief, the chart shows that home students tended to do better in Arts and Social Science-related subjects, whereas international students tended to do better in technology related subjects.

(163 words)

Unit 4

This is a response to a Type A 'Propose a solution to a problem' essay question.

This is a less emotive and therefore more academic way of saying *are destroyed*.

The writer begins with his least favoured option.

Notice that the writer does not use the contracted form *it's*.

Unit 4 – Task 2

In recent years there has been growing awareness of the importance of preserving the world's biological diversity. As increasing numbers of unique, and potentially useful, plants and animals come under threat, people are beginning to ask whether more can be done to reverse this trend.

One possible approach is to regulate agricultural and industrial activity so that pollution and disruption to natural habitats is kept to a minimum. People argue that economic prosperity must be curtailed if it comes at the expense of the environment. However, businesses affected are unlikely to comply with such a strategy. It may even generate hostility to conservation efforts generally if the economic costs are perceived to be too high.

An alternative approach would be to protect and expand nature reserves so that complete ecosystems can be kept intact. This would ensure that a minimum number of wild plants and animals would survive. However, although such places are indeed valuable, experience shows that it is difficult to protect rare plants and animals from exploitation. In fact, as some species, like the tiger, become rarer, the more valuable they become to poachers and others who seek to benefit from their trade.

A more effective approach is to educate the public about the benefits of biodiversity. Money should be invested in the research and development of the world's biological resources. Once people understand that there are real benefits to exploiting natural resources in a sustainable way, they are more likely to make the short-term sacrifices necessary to preserve natural habitats.

(253 words)

This is a more academic way of saying *more and more*.

The writer presents this idea impersonally by making *people* rather than *I* the subject of the sentence.

The writer concludes with his preferred option. This makes the essay feel finished. Notice how the writer avoids using the word *I* and keeps his sentences short and simple.

Unit 5 – Task 1

The introduction indicates what the diagram shows.

The diagram gives information about the five principal writing systems used throughout the world: the Logographic, Abjad, Abjuda, Alphabetic, and Syllabic.

Four of these are similar in that characters represent sounds. The oldest is the Abjad, used in Arabic, for example, where each character represents a consonant sound. Another is the Abjuda, used in the Indian Devanāgarī. Here, each character indicates a consonant plus vowel. The third system is the Alphabetic, used in English, for instance, where characters refer to a sound, either vowel or consonant. However, the relationship between pronunciation and spelling is sometimes approximate. Finally, in the Syllabic system, used in Japanese Kana for example, characters represent syllables.

The superlative form is used because more than two items are compared.

Another is used to signpost the second item in the list. Notice the remaining signposting expressions in this paragraph (*The third system* and *Finally*).

In addition to these four systems, there is also the Logographic system, which works on a different principle. Here, each character represents a word meaning. Therefore, languages which are different when spoken, such as Chinese and Japanese, can share written forms.

The concluding sentence says something about the diagram as a whole. The word *overall* signals the conclusion.

Overall, the diagram shows that most writing systems are based on sounds.

(167 words)

Unit 6

| This is a response to a type D 'Evaluate an idea' essay question. |
| An opposing point of view is given using the emphatic reporting verb *claim*. |
| This is the first generalisation, made less sweeping with the words *often* and *rather*. |

Unit 6 – Task 2

The Internet has undoubtedly changed the way people shop. In some countries, buying and selling products online has become commonplace. Enthusiasts claim that the Internet offers consumers greater choice and flexibility. However, those who say that the Internet is transforming the lives of consumers are going too far.

| In this part of the introduction, the writer describes the context of the topic. |
| The writer expresses his point of view by challenging the opposing point of view. |

Firstly, although online shopping appears to offer greater convenience, it is often rather risky and cumbersome in practice. Consumers cannot evaluate the quality of online products by handling them directly. Instead, they must rely on sellers to describe goods accurately in words and/or pictures. Mistakes can easily be made, leading to the inconvenience of having to exchange goods or seek a refund. Products bought online also normally need to be delivered by post. The convenience of online shopping thus hinges in part on the efficiency of the postal service.

Secondly, in spite of the promise of lower prices, Internet shopping seldom offers substantial savings. A competitive marketplace ensures that large price differentials rapidly disappear as suppliers align themselves with one another. Also, the cost of postage is normally borne by the buyer. A product that appears to be a bargain on screen often turns out to be no cheaper than the same product bought in a shop. Not surprisingly, only one in ten purchases in the UK are made online.

| This is the second generalisation, made less sweeping with the word *seldom*. |

| The writer gives his opinion (without using *I*). |
| The writer displays modesty by using the more tentative reporting verb *suggests*. |

For these reasons, Internet shopping is likely to remain a minority pursuit. The continuing popularity of shopping in the traditional way suggests that consumers continue to value its advantages: the opportunity to sample, compare and buy products in a real as opposed to a virtual space.

(265 words)

Unit 7 – Task 1

Figures 1 and 2 show economic growth and patterns of household expenditure from 1995 until 2010.

The introduction briefly summarises what the figures show.

In 1995, economic growth was approximately 1 per cent. The pie chart for that year shows that spending on essentials such as food and housing accounted for approximately two-thirds of total household expenditure. Spending on less essential items such as clothing, entertainment and travel was relatively modest at roughly 20 per cent.

This paragraph includes information from both figures. This pattern is repeated in the following paragraphs, which are sequenced chronologically.

In contrast highlights difference.

Five years later, growth had roughly doubled and expenditure on essentials had shrunk as a proportion of total spending. Spending on non-essentials, in contrast, had expanded. This trend was even more marked in 2005, when growth peaked at approximately 4.5 per cent and over 25 per cent of expenditure was devoted to non-essentials.

The comparative form (*more* + adjective) is used because two years are being compared.

The writer begins the paragraph with a generalisation.

However, the trend had reversed when in 2010 growth stood again at approximately 1 per cent following an economic contraction. The pattern of expenditure in that year was similar to the pattern in 1995, though the contraction in non-essential spending was even more pronounced.

Overall, the figures suggest that economic growth has an effect on patterns of household expenditure.

The conclusion cautiously expresses a cause-and-effect relationship between figures 1 and 2 using the less emphatic reporting verb *suggest*.

(169 words)

Unit 8

	Unit 8 – Task 2	
This is a response to a type A 'Propose a solution to a problem' question.	No two families are alike. Therefore, the degree of control that it is appropriate for parents to exercise over their 14–15-year-old adolescent children is likely to vary from family to family. In this essay, I will outline three key variables that should be considered when attempting to make a decision about what is suitable in a given context.	The writer states her opinion.
The writer's intention is expressed using *will*.		*Should* is used to express a necessity.
Each body paragraph begins with a generalisation.	One variable is the family's physical environment. Some environments clearly pose more dangers than others. Parents in an inner-city area with heavy traffic, a transient population and a high crime rate, for instance, probably need to supervise their children more closely than parents in a small rural community in which the residents know one-another.	This is a supporting example, signalled with *for instance*.
This supporting example is signalled with *for example*.	Secondly, prevailing cultural norms are likely to be a factor. Some cultures, in Asia and the Middle East, for example, value social cohesion, whereas others, such as the US, tend towards individualism. One of the tasks of parents is to teach their children to function within their society; thus the degree of parental control will probably vary according to the type of society in which children are expected to take part.	
	The third, and perhaps most important consideration, is the personalities of the children involved. Children vary enormously in terms of traits such as maturity, impulsiveness, conscientiousness, and so on. The degree of parental control appropriate for one 14–15-year-old may not be at all appropriate for another.	These examples are signalled with *such as*.
May is used to make the statement less sweeping.		
In short signals the conclusion.	In short, it is not possible to make recommendations regarding the supervision of adolescents that fit all contexts. The physical environment, the cultural context, and the personalities of those involved should all be considered.	The writer begins the conclusion by restating her opinion.
	(261 words)	Here the writer summarises the main points.

Unit 9

The colon is used to introduce a list.

The writer has organised this response chronologically, with all three trends compared in segments of time.

however is a sentence linker. It is usually punctuated with a full stop or semi colon before, and a comma after.

The writer uses the present perfect tense because the time frame is past to present.

This + summary word (trend) ensures cohesion.

Unit 9 – Task 1

The line graph shows three demographic trends in Scotland between 1940 and 2020: birth rate, population growth rate, and death rate.

Between 1940 and 1970, both birth rate and population growth rate fluctuated significantly. The birth rate started the period at 2.5 per cent and ended at just over 1.0 per cent. The population growth rate began and ended at approximately 1.0 per cent, having peaked at 1.5 per cent in 1955. The death rate, on the other hand, declined steadily until 1955 and then remained stable.

Between 1970 and 1990, all three trends declined gradually. In about 1990, the death rate overtook the population growth rate for the first time; however, all three trends remained roughly static over the next ten years.

Over the last decade, the birth rate and population growth rate have continued to decline, with the latter dipping below 0 per cent in 2005. The death rate, in contrast, has risen slightly. This trend is projected to continue over the next ten years.

(157 words)

both ... and links these trends.

on the other hand is a sentence linker signalling contrast. When placed after the subject of the sentence, it requires commas on either side.

with can be used as a cohesive device.

the latter is used to avoid repeating population growth rate.

This brief reference to the future is enough to make the passage feel complete. No separate conclusion is required.

Unit 10

This is a response to a type D 'Evaluate an idea' question.

Unit 10 – Task 2

Celebrities appear to play an increasingly prominent role in popular culture today. It is difficult to open a newspaper or switch on the television without encountering an item of celebrity gossip. Not surprisingly, there are concerns about how this trend impacts on children, with some people claiming that children are being corrupted. This essay will argue that these fears are unnecessarily alarmist.

this + summary word (*trend*) links two sentences.

This adverb phrase shows the writer's attitude to the opinion expressed.

Firstly, some people maintain that children cannot distinguish between notoriety and genuine fame. However, in my experience, children usually admire footballers, singers and actors for their skill and achievements and express disappointment when they misbehave. Moreover, historically famous figures have also been flawed. In the past, many prominent political and business leaders had links with the slave trade, for example. Yet they are still presented to children as noteworthy individuals.

The writer states her intention using *will*. The subject of the sentence is *this essay* rather than *I*, in keeping with academic style.

The writer avoids repeating *celebrities* by listing common types of celebrities.

Famous figures is used to avoid repetition.

Prominent and *noteworthy* in the following sentence are synonyms for famous.

Another common fear is that children are being encouraged to pursue the unrealistic goal of achieving celebrity status themselves instead of working towards more socially useful occupations such as engineering, teaching or nursing. In fact, children have always had unrealistic fantasies about what they might do as adults, and these commonly reflect the preoccupations of their society. In the 19th century, for example, British children often aspired to being famous explorers. As children grow up, they learn to draw inspiration from their heroes and heroines without emulating them literally.

These are examples of socially useful occupations, signalled with *such as*.

Commonly is a hedging expression, as is *often* in the following sentence.

In short, there is little about today's celebrity culture that is fundamentally more harmful than the types of celebrity children have encountered in the past. Provided children are given appropriate guidance, they are unlikely to be adversely affected.

Here, the conclusion begins with a summary of the main points.

(259 words)

Notice how the writer has paraphrased the task instructions.

Unit 11 – Task 1

The table compares four countries in terms of the proportion of journeys undertaken by five modes of travel: car, bicycle, public transport, walking, and 'other'. The bar chart gives findings of a study into the reasons people in the USA drive.

Of the four countries compared, the USA was heavily reliant on cars, with only a small proportion of journeys made by other means (only 10 per cent in total). The Netherlands, in contrast, showed a more even distribution of travel modes with fewer than half of all journeys made by car, a relatively large percentage made by bicycle (28 per cent) and nearly one in five on foot. France and the UK fell between these two extremes.

With is used as a cohesive device in this and the following sentence.

When the task requires you to compare several figures, the information must be more condensed.

Quantity is expressed in different ways. See also one in five in the following sentence.

The survey results shown in the bar chart may help explain why car use is higher in some countries than in others. The most cited reasons were the lack of alternative means of transport (38 per cent) and the need to use a car for work (28 per cent). However, convenience was also an important factor for over 20 per cent of respondents.

(172 words)

The paragraph begins with a generalisation.

A superlative is used as a focusing expression for the supporting detail that follows.

The response does not end with a general summary. However, at 172 words it is sufficiently long. It also feels complete as the two figures are adequately linked and described.

Unit 12

The writer makes reference to the opposing point of view to indicate that he has 'tested' his idea.

Each body paragraph begins with a generalisation.

This example supports the main point.

The writer signposts each key point.

This sentence summarises the main idea. Notice how the opposing point of view is expressed in the subordinate clause and the writer's view is expressed in the main clause. This gives the writer's view greater weight.

Unit 12 – Task 2

Human beings have long struggled with the difficulty of ensuring both freedom and fairness in society. Some people argue that a good society is necessarily one that ensures equality for all. However, in my view, this is neither feasible nor desirable in practice.

Firstly, it is difficult to define universal standards of achievement. For some, achievement means material success, for others it may mean something else: a simple but altruistic life, for example. Bill Gates and Mother Teresa were very different but both achieved a great deal. Because people define achievement in different ways, it is difficult to determine what equality of opportunity might mean in practice.

Secondly, people differ in terms of their talents. Some people can make the most of scanty resources; others do very little with inherited wealth or educational opportunities. Many highly successful individuals have had little of either in their early years, yet achieved a great deal. The relationship between equality of opportunity and personal success is not straightforward.

Finally, it is not easy to ensure a level playing field without damaging the incentive to do well. It is natural for parents to work hard in order to confer advantages on their children: private schooling, for example. It is difficult to see how equality of opportunity in education can be achieved without capping the aspirations of those who work hard.

In short, while equality of opportunity is an attractive concept, attempting to put this ideal into practice can do more harm than good. People are different in terms of their values, talents and initiative. It is not possible to ensure equality without distorting what makes people unique.

(273 words)

Some is used as a pronoun here to avoid repetition of people (see also others).

Each body paragraph ends with a concluding sentence which refers back to the key word equality. This repetition ensures good cohesion.

The writer maintains academic style by expressing his ideas impersonally. In this paragraph he uses a series of statements beginning It is + adjective.

The three main points of the body paragraphs are captured in the words values, talents and initiative.

Answer key

1   Gender roles

Part 1:   Vocabulary

Exercise 1
Suggested answers
Women d, e, g; Men a, b, c, f

Exercise 2
1 strengths   3 vulnerability   5 compliance
2 gentleness   4 authority   6 competition

Exercise 3
1 d,   2 a,   3 e,   4 f,   5 c,   6 b,   7 iv,   8 ii,
9 vi,   10 i,   11 vii,   12 v,   13 iii,   14 ix,   15 viii

Exercise 4
1 c,   2 e,   3 b,   4 a,   5 d

Part 2:   Practice exercises: Task 1

Exercise 1
1 20 minutes,   2 150 words,   3 No. You should select
and summarise the main features,   4 No

Exercise 2
1 a statement about the type of information shown
2 the fields which are dominated by men
3 the fields in which there are more equal numbers of
  men and women

4 makes a general statement about one of the main
  features of the chart
5 give supporting detail
6 a summary of the main features of the chart

Exercise 3
2 per cent should be *2 hours*;   *every day of the week*
should be *every weekday* (i.e. Monday–Friday)

Part 2:   Practice exercises: Task 2

Exercise 4
1 a,   2 b,   3 a,   4 a

Exercise 5
1 c,   2 a,   3 e,   4 d,   5 b
Questions: 1 approximately 50 words,   2 three,
3 three,   4 from weakest solution to strongest,
5 to emphasise your opinion and summarise the main points

Exercise 6
1 c: *Why do you think …?*
2 d: *Do you think … will …?*
3 b: *To what extent should …?*
4 a: *What can be done …?*
5 d: *Some people believe … because … What is your view
  …?*

Part 3: Exam practice

Task 1: Model answer

The bar chart gives information about male and female teachers in six types of educational institution in the UK in 2010. It shows what percentage of teachers were male and what percentage were female.

Women predominated in schools for children. This was particularly true of schools for very young children. Over 95 per cent of nursery school teachers, for example, were female. The situation was similarly one-sided in primary schools, where over 90 per cent of teachers were women.

Men and women were more equally represented in teaching institutions catering for older children and young adults: secondary schools and colleges. College lecturers, for example, were 50 per cent female and 50 per cent male.

Males held a larger share of teaching posts in higher-level institutions. This was particularly true for universities, where twice as many males were teaching staff than females.

Overall, women were more likely to hold the more typically maternal role of teaching young children. Males, on the other hand, predominated in the higher status teaching role of university lecturer.

Task 2: Model answer

There have always been differences in the types of work men and women have done. However, the trend in modern times has been for both men and women to have greater freedom of choice in terms of employment. Some people might say that there is no need to go further. However, in my view, wherever possible, gender equality should be encouraged.

There may indeed be good arguments for allowing certain posts to remain predominantly male or female. Where all-male or all-female groups exist, there may be a need for related posts to be held by men and women respectively. Patients in all-female hospital wards, for example, would probably appreciate having female nurses to look after them. It could also be argued that certain jobs requiring a great deal of physical strength, coal mining or logging, for example, should continue to be done mainly by men.

However, in the vast majority of situations, making occupations more open to both genders has distinct advantages. Men and women can bring slightly different perspectives and approaches to a job. Female police officers, for example, may have a greater understanding of domestic violence and a better range of strategies for dealing with this problem. Male primary school teachers probably have a better understanding of the needs of young boys and can serve as good role models for them.

The changes that result from allowing men into female-dominated occupations and vice versa may be subtle, but they are far-reaching. However, to benefit the most from this development, it is important not to expect males and females to approach work in identical ways.

2   Diet & nutrition

Part 1:   Vocabulary

Exercise 1
1 h,   2 g,   3 f,   4 i,   5 e,   6 b,   7 c,   8 a,   9 d

Exercise 2
1 b,   2 d,   3 a,   4 e,   5 g,   6 f,   7 h,   8 c

Exercise 3
1 increase   5 fall
2 peak   6 drop
3 decrease   7 fluctuation
4 dip

Exercise 4
1 d, e, g;   2 a, b, c, f

Exercise 5
1 decreased dramatically   4 dropped significantly
2 dipped modestly   5 fluctuated moderately
3 fell slightly

Part 2:   Practice exercises: Task 1

Exercise 1
Past tense: rose, leveled off, was, reached;

Present perfect tense: has fluctuated;

Expressions which refer to the future: is expected to, is also projected to

1 Use the past tense when describing a trend or event that happened between two fixed times in the past.
2 Use the present perfect tense to describe a trend or event that started at a fixed time in the past and has continued until the present.
3 Other expressions that you can use to describe future trends include: *is/are likely to* and *is/are predicted to*. Note: You should avoid using *will*.
4 Use the present tense when describing a cyclical trend, for example a trend that happens in the same way every year.

Exercise 2
1 increased/rose,   2 dramatically/sharply/steeply,   3 peaked,   4 remained the same,   5 has been,   6 dramatic/sharp/steep,   7 expected/projected/likely/predicted,   8 increase/rise,   9 gradually/moderately/modestly

Exercise 3
1 c,   2 a,   3 d,   4 e,   5 b,   6 e

Exercise 4
Description 1
The percentage of obese adults rose steadily from 8 per cent in 1950 to 15 per cent in 1970. There was a slight dip, <u>and then there was</u> a gradual rise until 1990. <u>It rose</u> steeply for the next ten years, <u>and then</u> it levelled off. It has risen even more sharply, <u>and</u> it is projected to peak at 35 per cent in 2010, <u>and then it will</u> level off.

Description 2

The percentage of obese adults rose steadily from 8 per cent in 1950 to 15 per cent in 1970. There was a slight dip, followed by a gradual rise until 1990. After rising steeply for the next ten years, it levelled off. Since then, it has risen even more sharply. It is projected to peak at 35 per cent in 2010, and level off thereafter.

Note: If you are aiming for a Band 6.5+, you should avoid using *and* too much.
Use *followed by* + adjective + noun.
Use *after* + *-ing* instead of subject + finite verb, but remember, you must have a subject in the main clause that follows.
Example: *After rising steeply ..., it levelled off.*
If you list one verb after another, you only need to write the subject for the first verb.
Example: *It rose sharply, then fell, then levelled off.*

> **Model answer**
>
> Between 1996 and 1999, expenditure on convenience foods fell gradually from approximately £25 per week to half that amount. *After rising sharply over the next three years, it* levelled off at £30 per week. It remained the same for over two years. *There was a brief dip, followed by a slight rise.* Between 2005 and 2007 it fluctuated. *Then, after rising sharply, it* peaked at nearly £50 per week in 2008. *Since* then it has fallen.

Part 2: Practice exercises: Task 2

Exercise 5
All answers valid

Exercise 6
1 c, e, g;   2 a, b, d, f

Exercise 7
1 b,   2 c,   3 d,   4 a,   5 e,   6 h,   7 g,   8 f

Exercise 8
Suggested answers
1 People who are too concerned with being slim could be considered vain.
2 It is healthier to be slim.
3 People who are overweight are more likely to suffer from health problems such as heart disease and diabetes.
4 Many people underestimate the amount of calories in food.
5 Some people cannot lose weight even if they know what is in their food and how much they should eat.
6 Obesity may be due to genetic factors.
7 People who are related tend to have similar body shapes and sizes.
8 This does not explain why obesity rates are rising in modern times.

Part 3:   Exam practice

Task 1: Model answer

Over the past fifty years, there has been significant variation in the percentage of young people in the UK who choose to eat a vegetarian diet.

In 1960, only a small percentage of adolescents (about 1 per cent) were vegetarian. There was then a steep increase until 1978, when over 15 per cent were following a vegetarian diet. Thereafter, the percentage fell steadily until 1990 and then fluctuated for a decade. It reached a low point of just 4 per cent in 1996. It has risen gradually since 2000 and is expected to continue to do so over the next few years. After reaching a high point in around 2015, it is projected to decline again and possibly level off by the decade's end.

Overall, the graph shows two main periods of interest in vegetarianism among young people in the UK: one peaking around 1978 and the second projected to peak approximately forty years later, in 2015.

Task 2: Model answer

The increasing availability of convenience foods has been a significant feature of modern life in many developed countries. Some people have predicted that with advances in food technology, traditional foods and traditional methods of food preparation will disappear. In this essay, I will argue that this is unlikely to happen.

It is true that nowadays many people do not have enough time to cook and that convenience foods present an attractive option. These foods have improved significantly in terms of quality and availability and the range for sale in the average supermarket is quite impressive. It is possible to find even very sophisticated ready-prepared microwavable meals.

However, the growing popularity of television cookery programmes, 'celebrity chefs', and cook books suggest that people continue to value traditional ways of preparing foods. Farmers markets selling fresh, locally-produced food continue to be the norm in many parts of the world. In fact, they are growing in popularity in countries such as the UK, where they had virtually disappeared from many cities. This may be partly because cooking with basic, natural ingredients is cheaper than buying processed foods.

Moreover, traditional foods are an important aspect of culture and social life. In many countries, traditional meals continue to be shared in regular family gatherings. Important celebrations such as weddings, Christmas and Chinese New Year are marked by traditionally prepared feasts.

In spite of the utility of convenience foods, people are unlikely to abandon practices that are economically sound and give them great pleasure. It is hard to imagine a world in which people do not continue to enjoy traditional, home-cooked meals at least some of the time.

3 Educational goals

Part 1: Vocabulary

Exercise 1
a 2, b 8, c 1, d 5, e 4, f 6, g 3, h 7

Exercise 2
1 rote learning	4 higher education
2 critical thinking	5 continuous assessment
3 formal examinations	6 educational standards

Exercise 3
i c, ii a, iii f, iv b, v d, vi e

Exercise 4
1 a small minority	4 nearly half
2 the vast majority	5 roughly one in four
3 just under a third	6 three quarters

Part 2: Practice exercises: Task 1

Exercise 1
1 as … as	3 least	5 higher
2 lower	4 fewer	6 lowest

Exercise 2
1 D: *On the other hand*   3 S: *similar*
2 D: *Whereas*   4 S: *both*

Exercise 3
1 Fewer boys than girls passed their English examination.
2 As many boys as girls achieved a passing grade in Mathematics.
3 Whereas boys did well in Technology, girls did well in language-related subjects.
4 The number of passes in Religious Studies was lower for boys than for girls.
5 Similar numbers of boys and girls passed the Economics exam.

Part 2: Practice exercises: Task 2

Exercise 4
1 Type a: propose a solution
2 The writer has omitted: *Students would make more friends; Some projects would be poor quality; It's better for students to be in classrooms because that's what people expect; Some teachers wouldn't be good at this.* She has omitted them because these points are not strictly relevant to the issue of how teamwork can be encouraged and assessed.
3 The points are arranged from weakest to strongest, with critical evaluation of each point leading logically to the next point. This allows the writer to make a strong conclusion.
4 The writer wants to present this suggestion as stronger than the previous two suggestions.

Exercise 5: Suggested ideas
1 People often perform poorly in examinations because they are anxious, not because they lack intelligence.
2 Many people who do poorly in exams are successful in fields that clearly require intelligence, e.g. technology or business.
3 There is probably no definitive proof of whether there is one kind of intelligence or several kinds of intelligence.

Example essay outline

Introduction:	Measuring intelligence is a difficult task
Body paragraph 1:	**Idea in the question** –Exams measure intelligence
	Evidence for: people who do well in exams often do well in other types of tasks, e.g. assignments; exams usually include a range of tasks to measure different abilities
	Evidence against: pen & paper exams are often predictable – students can prepare by rote learning; people often perform poorly in examinations because they are anxious, not because they lack intelligence
Body paragraph 2:	**Other possible idea:** there are probably different types of intelligence – these can only be measured in different ways
	Evidence against: there is probably no definitive proof of whether there is one kind of intelligence or several kinds of intelligence
	Evidence for: some people express themselves much better verbally than in writing; many people who did poorly in exams, are successful in fields that clearly require intelligence, e.g. technology, business
Conclusion:	'pen and paper' exams probably useful for measuring certain kinds of intelligence, but have limitations; other methods needed

Exercise 6: Suggested ideas

Template B: 'Evaluate the solution' essay questions		
What are the possible solutions?	**Positive consequence(s)**	**Drawback(s)**
Solution in the question: cram schools	give students the opportunity to practise taking exams students get support many students who attend such schools do well in exams	teach students to be 'test wise' rather than to learn can be stressful unfair because they give advantage to students who can afford to pay
Other possible solution: vary the format of exams and match them to what is taught in schools	if students pay attention in school, there is no need for additional cramming in countries with exams that properly reflect the curriculum, there are few cram schools fair for everyone	some people will always want to get ahead & there will always be businesses that want to exploit that desire

Example essay outline

Introduction:	cram schools are big business; may not be a good thing
Body paragraph 1:	solution in the question – cram schools serve a need
	evidence for: give students opportunity to practise; students get support; many students who attend such schools do well in exams
	evidence against: teach students to be 'test wise' rather than to learn; can be stressful; unfair because they give advantage to students who can afford to pay
Body paragraph 2:	**other possible solution** – vary the format of exams and match them to what is taught
	evidence against: some people will always want to get ahead & there will always be businesses that want to exploit that desire
	evidence for: if students pay attention in school, there is no need for additional cramming; in countries with good exams that properly reflect the curriculum, there are few cram schools; fair for everyone
Conclusion:	cram schools are a symptom of a faulty educational system

Exercise 7: Suggested headings

Introduction:	
Body paragraph 1:	Idea 1 ('weakest idea')
	Evidence for:
	Evidence against:
Body paragraph 2:	Idea 2 ('better idea')
	Evidence for:
	Evidence against:
Body paragraph 3:	Idea 3 ('best idea')
	Evidence for:
Conclusion:	

Note: The outlines suggested in this unit are useful for most Task 2 questions. For some Task 2 questions, you may want or need to modify them. For example, you may want to discuss two rather than three ideas or solutions. On occasion, you may need to combine elements of two types of outline, for example if you are asked to discuss an idea *and* propose a solution to a problem.

Part 3: Exam practice

Task 1: Model answer
The bar chart shows the proportion of UK students and international students achieving second class degrees or higher in seven different subjects at a university in the UK.

Degree results were generally good for both home and international students, with well over 50 per cent gaining a second class degree or better in all seven subjects except International Law. International students tended to do better than UK students in technology-related subjects. This was particularly true of Information Technology. Whereas over 80 per cent of international students gained a good degree in IT, only about half of the UK students did so.

Degree results were similar for the two groups in Nursing and Accounting. In Arts and Social Science-related subjects, UK students tended to do better. The biggest gap in performance was in International Law, where three-quarters of UK students gained a second class degree or better. In contrast, fewer than half of the international students attained this level.

Overall, the chart suggests that international and UK students had different strengths when studying for degrees in this UK university.

Task 2: Model answer
Examinations are one of the most common methods of measuring learning in education systems throughout the world. At virtually every stage of the learning process, exams are used to verify that the learner is ready to move on to the next stage. However, many people believe that the role of examinations should be reconsidered.

There are clearly certain advantages to exams. They help to ensure fairness by imposing the same conditions on all exam candidates. They are also relatively versatile; different types of exam questions, for example, multiple-choice questions and essay tasks, can test different sorts of reasoning ability. However, exams also have clear drawbacks. Test-wise candidates can often perform well on exams without having good underlying knowledge or skills. On the other hand, some test-takers perform poorly in exams simply because of anxiety. Some teachers and learners focus only on those aspects of the curriculum that are likely to be tested, thus narrowing the educational experience for all.

A number of measures should be taken to address these concerns. Wherever possible, exams should match the content and activities of the learning environment. Exam tasks should be varied to give fair opportunities to candidates with different types of skills. Other types of assessment should also be considered; assignment writing, for example, to assess independent learning and research skills, or group projects, to measure teamwork ability.

Exams clearly have a role to play in ensuring proper, objective assessment of achievement. However, exams need to be carefully designed and supplemented with other forms of assessment if they are to be a truly useful component of the educational system.

4 Biodiversity

Part 1: Vocabulary

Exercise 1
a 2, b 1, c 6, d 5, e 3, f 4

Exercise 2
1 b, 2 e, 3 d, 4 f, 5 a, 6 g, 7 c

Exercise 3
1 Sentences 1, 2, 3, 5, 6
2 Sentences 4, 7
3 *Contribute to* implies there is more than one cause.

Exercise 4
1 Intensive farming has contributed to a significant decline in biodiversity.
2 Vegetation has been lost; consequently, the insect population has declined.
3 There are fewer insects, so the small animals that feed on them have moved elsewhere.
4 There has been a marked reduction in numbers of predators such as wild cats and owls because of the disappearance of prey species.

Exercise 5
1 damaged	4 used
2 are endangered	5 limit
3 loss	

Part 2: Practice exercises: Task 1

Exercise 1
a pioneer plants,   b gather moisture,
c return organic material to the soil,   d shrubs

 i the active voice
ii the passive voice

Exercise 2
1 They provide shade, gather moisture and return organic material to the soil.
2 They quickly cover the ground, crowding out the pioneers.
3 However, they too eventually die off as young trees push through the brush.
4 The logs are then sorted by size and loaded onto logging trucks for transport to the sawmill.
5 Once the trees have been extracted, they are processed by chain saw.

Exercise 3
beginning stages: *Firstly, first*
middle stages: *Secondly, then, In the second phase*
end stages: *In the final stage, finally*

Exercise 4
2 slows	7	grows
3 is/becomes	8	are caught
4 forms	9	are cut
5 is reduced	10	is lost
6 decreases		

Exercise 5

Suggested answers

b Because flooding is less frequent, the quantity of nutrients on land and agricultural output decrease.

c A sand bar forms across the estuary; as a result, salinity in the estuary decreases.

d As salinity in the estuary decreases, fewer fish are caught.

e Due to the growth of the human population and smaller fish catches, mangrove trees are cut.

f Once the mangrove trees are/have been cut, mangrove cover in the estuary is lost.

Suggested answer

First, a dam is constructed at the river head, slowing the flow of water. Secondly, because flooding is less frequent, the quantity of nutrients on land and agricultural output decrease. A sand bar forms across the estuary; as a result, salinity in the estuary decreases. As salinity decreases, fewer fish are caught. Finally, due to population growth and smaller fish catches, the mangrove trees are cut. Once they have been cut, mangrove cover in the estuary is lost.

Part 2:   Practice exercises: Task 2

Exercise 6

Response 1

If you look at it that way, it's true that humans and animals have conflicting interests. People have always exploited animals for food and clothing, and farmers have brought bigger and bigger areas of wild land under cultivation. But should we keep on doing this?

   In regions of the world where the population is growing, and there aren't enough resources, the conflict between humans and animals is really bad. If you go to Africa, for example, you can see large nature reserves alongside really poor human settlements. I love the idea of elephants and lions living in the wild. But often it's the poor farmer living nearby who's got to pay the cost in terms of land and lost earnings.

Response 2

Looked at from a broad historical perspective, it is true that humans and animals have had conflicting interests. People have always exploited animals for food and clothing, whilst farmers have brought ever increasing areas of wild land under cultivation. Whether this process should continue is a question that requires careful consideration.

   In regions of the world where the population is growing and resources are scarce, the conflict between humans and animals is particularly problematic. This can be seen in parts of Africa, for example, where large nature reserves sit alongside very poor human settlements. People living thousands of miles away may value the idea of elephants and lions living in the wild. However, often it is the poor farmer living nearby who must pay the cost in terms of land and lost earnings.

1 Response 1 is informal in style; Response 2 is academic in style.

2 Response 2 is more impersonal and less emotional. There are fewer conjunctions and more subordinators. There are no colloquialisms or contracted forms.

Exercise 7

Characteristics of academic style	Examples from the texts	
	Informal style	Academic style
Academic style is more impersonal. Avoid overusing personal pronouns (*I, you, we*) and addressing the reader directly.	*If you look at it that way,* *But should we keep on doing this?* *If you go to Africa, …, you can see* *I love*	*Looked at from a broad historical perspective,* *Whether this process should continue is a question that requires careful consideration.* *This can be seen in parts of Africa* *People living thousands of miles away may value*
Academic style is less emotional. Avoid exaggeration (*totally, perfect*), emotive words (*terrible, adore*) and words that express value judgments (*immoral*).	*bad* *love*	*problematic* *may value*
Academic style uses fewer conjunctions (*and, but*) and more subordinators (*whereas, because*) and sentence linkers (*nevertheless, therefore*).	*and farmers* *But often it's the poor farmer*	*whilst farmers* *However, it is often the poor farmer*
Academic style uses different vocabulary. Avoid colloquial expressions, phrasal verbs (*take up, break out*), double comparatives (*more and more*), contacted forms (*isn't, won't*) and the words *get, lots of, a lot of,* and *really*.	*It's* *bigger and bigger areas* *really bad* *really poor human settlements* *who's got to pay*	*It is* *increasing areas* *particularly problematic* *very poor human settlements* *who must pay*

Exercise 8

Model answer

However, in relation to plants, the advantages of conservations are more apparent. It is important to remember that wild plants are not just things of beauty; they are also a very valuable resource. Wild plants have been used throughout history to make medicines like aspirin. Also, if certain varieties of crops are prone to disease, wild plants could be used to develop new varieties. Because there are many plants that have not yet been discovered, their potential uses remain unknown.

To sum up, in my view, it is worth trying to preserve natural habitats because wild animals and plants are unique and could save lives. However, it is important to remember that people's basic needs have to be met too. Therefore, the burden of protecting plant and animal species should be distributed fairly.

Exercise 9
Suggested answers
1 It could be argued that the desire for wealth encourages people to exploit the environment.
2 Environmental degradation may be unavoidable because there is no way of enforcing international agreements. Leaders may sign such agreements simply to create a favourable impression in the media.

Part 3: Exam practice

Task 1: Model answer

The flow chart shows what typically occurs as a consequence of deforestation. When trees are removed, there are four main immediate effects, which eventually result in flooding, degraded vegetation and a loss of biodiversity.

One immediate effect is soil which has been compacted by heavy equipment. The resulting hard, 'baked' soil contributes to the run off of rain water and, eventually, flooding.

Another immediate consequence of logging is a reduction in the number of roots holding the soil together. This leads to soil erosion. As a consequence, the quality and variety of vegetation is compromised.

The third immediate effect is burning, both deliberate and as a consequence of an increased risk of forest fires. The waste that remains after logging is destroyed and the microorganisms that feed on this material are lost. This leads to degraded vegetation.

The final immediate consequence is a reduction in the amount of moisture plants return to the air. Because there is less moisture in the air, there is less precipitation and an increased incidence of drought. This too reduces plant growth and ultimately results in degraded vegetation and a loss of biodiversity.

Task 2: Model answer

As natural resources come under increasing pressure, the list of endangered plants and animals continues to grow. The causes are many: developments in agriculture, mining, forestry and transport. Some would argue that the loss of biodiversity is a price we must pay for progress. In my view, however, there is much that governments can and should do to protect the world's plants and animals.

Governments could promote greater understanding of plants and animals by investing in the research and preservation efforts of universities, zoos, and botanical institutes. This may ensure the survival of individual species and produce tangible benefits in the form of new medicines and products. However, this strategy alone would do little to protect whole ecosystems that are under threat.

An alternative strategy would be to protect natural habitats by expanding nature reserves. This would have immediate positive consequences for those areas by preserving delicate ecosystems. However, this strategy also has limitations. It does not protect from phenomena such as acid rain and water pollution, which can cross boundaries and affect large areas.

The most effective solution is to limit the damage at its source. Companies that engage in practices that harm the environment should be required to demonstrate that they have taken all reasonable efforts to minimise the damage. Public contracts for roads and buildings should only be awarded to firms that have a good environmental track record.

The strategies outlined above: preservation, protection and, above all prevention, can do much to reverse the destruction that threatens the world's plants and animals. The aesthetic and practical benefits of doing so are well worth the cost.

5 Global English

Part 1: Vocabulary

Exercise 1
1 e, 2 g, 3 b, 4 c, 5 f, 6 a, 7 h, 8 d

Exercise 2
1 c, 2 f, 3 e, 4 g, 5 b, 6 d, 7 a

Exercise 3
1 insist	5 urge
2 refute	6 maintain
3 deny	7 dismiss
4 advocate	

Exercise 4
1 I concede that making English a mandatory subject in primary schools is not a good idea.
2 Some people insist that the world needs one common language for trade.
3 I refute the idea that everyone in the world will speak the same language at any point in the future.
4 Teachers recommend practising a foreign language outside of the classroom in order to become fluent.

Part 2: Practice exercises: Task 1

Exercise 1

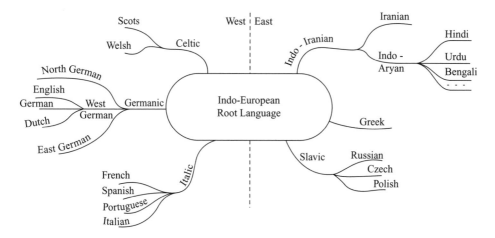

Exercise 2
Order: c, d, a, b

1 The first and fourth paragraphs make generalisations about the whole diagram. The second and third paragraphs give specific information about parts of the diagram.
2 The introduction indentifies the type of information shown by the diagram; the conclusion makes a general statement about the information.
3 General to specific
4 Suggested answers: The diagram shows (that); there are two main branches; in addition to … it includes; it comprises

Exercise 3

1 b

2 c

3 It repeats the words in the task instructions.

4 It has too much detailed information.

Exercise 4

Suggested answers

1 The bar chart shows the proportion of children in European secondary schools who are studying five different foreign languages in the years 1990, 2000 and 2010.

2 In summary, the figure shows that some of the more dominant world languages, English in particular, are being more widely taught, whereas other languages, with the exception of Spanish, are becoming less popular.

Part 2: Practice exercises: Task 2

Exercise 5

1 c/b, 2 b, 3 d, 4 e

1 It begins with the context and ends with the writer's opinion.

2 The last position makes the sentence more prominent.

Exercise 6

1 e, 2 e, 3 b, 4 g, 5 d

Order: 3, 5, 2, 1, 4

Exercise 7

1 d, 2 e, 3 c, 4 a, 5 f, 6 b

Exercise 8

Model answers

1 It is very likely that the spread of English as a lingua franca is connected in some way with the process of globalisation. Some people believe that because language is an aspect of culture, speaking a particular language involves adopting some of the values of that culture. In this essay I will examine the arguments for and against this view.

2 As anyone who has travelled abroad will know, misunderstandings can easily occur among people from different cultures. It is sometimes assumed that this happens because the people involved do not have an adequate knowledge of the language. However, I would argue that more than language knowledge is required to communicate successfully. This essay will examine what I believe to be the most important factors in communication breakdown.

Part 3: Exam practice

Task 1: Model answer

The diagram illustrates six different writing systems.

There is one type of writing system, the Logographic, in which characters represent word meanings. An example of this is Chinese. Interestingly, because each character represents a word meaning rather than a sound, it is possible for two languages which are different in spoken form to share the same writing system. This is partially the case with Chinese and Japanese, for example.

There are four types of writing system in which characters represent sounds. The oldest of these is the Abjad, in which each character represents a consonant sound. Arabic uses this type of system. Related to this is the Abjuda system, in which each character represents a consonant plus a vowel sound. The third type, the Alphabetic system, is slightly different in that consonant and vowel sounds are represented by different characters. English, for example, uses this type of system. Finally the Syllabic system is used in languages such as Japanese Kana, in which there are a relatively small number of possible syllables in the spoken form.

Overall, the diagram shows that there is wide variation in writing systems around the world.

Task 2: Model answer

As the world becomes more integrated, the need for common means of communication is becoming more pressing. Inevitably, speakers of minority languages have been under pressure to speak the languages of more dominant groups, both locally and globally. Some people argue that there is nothing that can or should be done to stop this process. I would suggest that the issue merits more careful consideration.

It is true that as the balance of power among groups of people throughout history has shifted, languages have arisen, changed, and died out. Even once widely-spoken languages, such as Latin, have disappeared. To some extent, therefore, this process may be inevitable. However, there are examples of communities that have managed to preserve and even revive languages under threat. Irish and Scots Gaelic, for example, have been preserved by government policy on education and broadcast media.

There are, indeed, several benefits to preserving minority languages. Retaining the language of a community often means that other forms of culture are maintained: songs, literature and local traditions. These all contribute to the richness and variety of human culture. Moreover, language helps communities to remain cohesive and to have a strong sense of identity. This can help people to be strong in adversity. Where this sense of identity and cohesion has been lost, for example among many indigenous communities in North America, problems can follow: low self-esteem, lack of confidence and loss of initiative.

In short, it is possible and in many cases, desirable, to make the effort to preserve minority languages. This can have benefits both for the minority speech community and for society as a whole in terms of cultural richness.

6   The Internet

Part 1:   Vocabulary

Exercise 1
a 3, b 5, c 2, d 1, e 6, f 4

Exercise 2
a vi, b iv, c ii, d iii, e v, f i

Exercise 3
1 noticeable
2 distinctive
3 underlying
4 main
5 widespread

Exercise 4
a 2, b 6, c 3, d 5, e 1, f 4

Exercise 5
1 advances
2 advent
3 enables
4 trend
5 accelerating
6 devices

Part 2:   Practice exercises: Task 1

Exercise 1
1 Response 2 is more satisfactory. In Response 1, the writer has simply reproduced the information in the table in words, whereas in Response 2, the writer has highlighted the significance of the data by emphasising main points and supporting these with detailed information from the table.
2 The first and last sentences contain main points in both responses *(The table shows that … Overall …)*. In Response 2, the first line of paragraph 2 *(The most significant change was …)* and the first line of paragraph 3 *(Another noticeable trend …)* also contain general statements.
3 In Response 1, there is a general introductory statement followed by several detailed points, ending with a general concluding statement. In Response 2, there are four general statements, each followed by supporting details.

Exercise 2
1 There has been significant growth in Internet use worldwide; Internet users now make up nearly 30 per cent of the population. The most significant figure is probably the percentage change (455 per cent).
2 The most significant groupings are (a) developing regions (Africa, Asia, the Middle East, and Latin America) and (b) developed regions (Europe, North America, and Australia).
3 The developed regions have the largest percentages of Internet users – all over 50 per cent. The developing regions have the smallest – all under 50 per cent.
4 The developing regions have all experienced the highest rates of growth in Internet users. The developed regions have experience the lowest rates of growth.

Exercise 3
Suggested answers
1 One significant trend is the high percentage of Internet users in the most economically developed regions of the world. Seventy-eight per cent of the population of North America, for example, use the Internet. Nearly two-thirds of Australians and Europeans are also Internet users.

2 The smallest growth in the percentage of Internet users occurred in the most developed regions of the world. Growth in North America, which had the highest percentage of Internet users, was the lowest at 137 per cent. Australia and Europe also experienced relatively low percentage increases in Internet users at 181 per cent and 353 per cent respectively.

3 Another noticeable feature of the information in the table is the relatively low percentage of Internet users in the least developed regions of the world. Less than one third of the populations of Africa, Asia, the Middle East, and Latin America use the Internet. The region with the smallest percentage of Internet users was Africa at 10 per cent.

4 However, the biggest growth in Internet users occurred in developing regions. The percentage of the population online in Africa, for instance, grew nearly twenty-five fold. The Middle East and Latin America also saw Internet use grow more than ten fold.

Part 2:   Practice exercises: Task 2

Exercise 4
Strengths: (1) It has a clear structure. (2) There are good supporting examples for each of the two main points.

Weaknesses: (1) The main points repeat parts of the essay question. (2) It follows a typical formula and does not show strong skills in essay organisation.

Exercise 5
1 The Internet has the potential to diminish family life but also to enhance it. Supporting points: b, e
2 Similarly, the Internet can distract people from spending time with their friends; however, it can also help people make and keep friends. Supporting points: a, d, f
3 In work situations, the Internet can rob workers of time for face-to-face contact, but it can also make it easier to work together. Supporting points: c, g

The main advantage of this plan is that it shows a more sophisticated structure: the advantages and disadvantages of the Internet are discussed in relation to three main themes: family, friends and work.

Exercise 6
1 The second sentence is more appropriate because it is less sweeping and, therefore, easier to defend as valid.
2 You could modify the first sentences is several ways:

Excessive Internet use *sometimes* leads to social isolation. (frequency adverb)

Excessive Internet use *possibly* leads to social isolation. (probability adverb)

It is said that excessive Internet use leads to social isolation. (expressions)

Excessive Internet use *appears to lead to* social isolation. (less absolute language)

Exercise 7
Suggested answers
1 Many people over the age of fifty have difficulty grasping new technology.
2 People often want to own the latest gadget.
3 The Internet can sometimes have a harmful effect on children.
4 Some people do not like new technology because they find it difficult to understand.
5 Too much technology may make some people less active.
6 It is possible that some of the world's problems may be alleviated by advances in science and technology.

Exercise 8
Suggested outline of body paragraphs:

1 Illiteracy a major obstacle (G)

   In some countries, less than 50 per cent population able to read (S)

   Women & the poor especially likely to be illiterate (S)

2 Basic infrastructure inadequate (G)

   Electricity supply irregular (S)

   Broadband access only in major cities (S)

3 Even where IT access available, governments fearful of well-informed public (G)

   Government censorship of Internet widespread (S)

   Use of blocking software & firewalls common (S)

Model answer

People who live in developed countries often take access to information technology for granted. However, as the IT revolution moves forward in some parts of the world, elsewhere the disadvantaged are falling further and further behind. Indeed there are many barriers to wider IT access and its potential benefits.

In many parts of the world, illiteracy remains a major obstacle to IT access. In some countries, less than 50 per cent of the population is able to read. Women and the poor are especially likely to be illiterate and therefore at a disadvantage when it comes to IT access and its potential benefits.

Another major barrier is inadequate infrastructure. In some countries, the electricity supply is irregular. In addition, broadband may only be available in major cities, rendering many rural areas off the map as far as IT access is concerned. In these circumstances, the Internet may actually be increasing rather than decreasing social inequality between urban and rural areas.

Even where IT access is available, governments are often fearful of a well-informed public. In fact, government censorship of the Internet is widespread. The use of blocking software and firewalls is common, even in countries such as Australia, which are commonly regarded as free and democratic. Those who are well-educated and sophisticated may be able to find a way around such obstacles; however, those who are less advantaged may remain unable to access some information freely.

In short, where unequal access to infrastructure, education and free information exist, the IT revolution is unlikely to reduce inequality. Unless fundamental inequalities are addressed, the Internet may, in fact, increase social divides.

Part 3: Exam practice

7 Consumer spending

Part 1: Vocabulary

Exercise 1
1 e, 2 b, 3 d, 4 a, 5 f, 6 c, 7 h, 8 g

Exercise 3
1 d, 2 c, 3 e, 4 f, 5 a, 6 b

Exercise 2
1 disposable income
2 personal debt
3 goods and services
4 consumer confidence
5 household expenditure

Exercise 4
1 c, 2 f, 3 g, 4 a, 5 d, 6 b, 7 e

Part 2: Practice exercises: Task 1

Exercise 1
1 Both figures relate to consumer spending.
2 C – cause and effect
3 If you look at the overall trends, you may notice a connection between the disposable income of the three age groups and the sales figures for the products most likely to be purchased by people in these age groups. Any obvious points, for example, peaks and low points that help to illustrate the connection should be highlighted.
4 You could use either, though you can highlight the connection between age and sales of certain products most effectively by comparing features of both figures in each paragraph.

Exercise 2
1 The first sentence gives a description of what is shown in figure 1; the second sentence gives a description of what is shown in figure 2; the third sentence makes a statement about the relationship between figures 1 and 2.
2 Cause and effect: *Seen together, the figures suggest a link between …*
3 In paragraph 1, the writer describes the overall trend in disposable income for 15–24 year-olds, then the overall trend in sales for the products most likely to be purchased by that age group.
In paragraph 2, the writer describes the overall trend in disposable income for 35–44 year-olds, then the overall trend in sales for the products most likely to be purchased by that age group.
In paragraph 3, the writer describes the overall trend in disposable income for 65–74 year-olds, then the overall trend in sales for the products most likely to be purchased by that age group.
4 The writer focuses on peaks in both trends because this is sufficient to demonstrate that there is a connection.
5 *showed a similar pattern*, *with*; *also*; *not surprisingly … also*
6 *may be influenced by*

Exercise 3
Suggested answers
1 When the availability of cheap credit increases, consumer spending increases; when the availability of cheap credit decreases, consumer spending decreases.
2 When the rate of taxation increases, consumer spending decreases; when the rate of taxation decreases, consumer spending increases.
The two figures show that:
a The rate of taxation is inversely proportional to levels of consumer spending.
b The availability of cheap credit is proportional to levels of consumer spending.
c When the availability of cheap credit rises, levels of consumer spending also appear to rise.
d When the rate of taxation falls, levels of consumer spending appear to rise.
e The less consumers are taxed, the more they spend.
f The more cheap credit is available, the more consumers spend.

Exercise 4
Suggested answer
Figure 1 shows the percentage change in the amount of credit available and taxation between 1990 and 2010. The second figure shows the percentage increase in expenditure on three different types of products at five-year intervals over the same time period.

Seen together, the two figures suggest that there is a positive correlation between the availability of credit and levels of consumer spending. The availability of credit reached a peak in 2005, when nearly 60 per cent more credit was available than in 1990. Spending on all three categories of products (food, household appliances and clothing) also reached a peak.

On the other hand, the level of consumer spending appears to be inversely proportional to the rate of taxation. When taxation fell sharply in the periods leading up to 1995 and 2005, consumer spending appeared to increase sharply.

Overall, greater availability of credit appears to act as a stimulus to consumer spending, whereas higher taxation may have the opposite effect.

Part 2: Practice exercises: Task 2

Exercise 5
1 Response 2 is more satisfactory because it contains examples to illustrate and support the main point. Response 1 essentially repeats the main point in three different ways.
2 to state the main point
3 Sentence 2 further explains the main point, sentence 3 gives an example to illustrate the main point, sentence 4 supports the main point.
4 *An example of this*
5 *Indeed*

Exercise 6
1 *for example* or *for instance*
2 *Another good example of this*
3 *indeed* or *in fact*

Exercise 7
Suggested answers
1 Some people buy products that they do not really need because they feel empty and unhappy. For instance, people often consume alcohol, cigarettes or sugary foods because these enhance mood. Indeed, the link between emotion and buying is evident in the fact that much of the content of advertisements has little to do with giving factual information about the product being promoted.
2 People often buy products they do not really need because they want to display their status or wealth. A good example of this is when people dispose of perfectly good items (clothing, furniture, electronic goods) simply to buy a more up-to-date model. Another example is when shoppers choose high-value brands that prominently display their logos over anonymous brands that are equivalent in quality but cheaper. Indeed, the relationship between social status and consumer spending is so powerful that many brands are carefully targeted at particular social groups.
3 Sometimes people buy products they do not really need because they want to use them in a positive way to make their lives more enjoyable or interesting. In an ideal world, all people would have some disposable income with which to buy products or services that enhance their lives in some way. Hobbies, music and novels, for example, are all products that are not strictly necessary for survival, but can contribute greatly to quality of life.

Exercise 8
Suggested answer
It is likely that financial institutions are at least partially responsible for high levels of personal debt. In times when lenders are less tightly regulated and greater competition is allowed, there is a natural tendency to try to attract more customers by making it easier to borrow money. Banks may choose to lend to people who have relatively low incomes or who already have high levels of personal debt. This practice may be sustainable up to a point; however, when the economy suffers and people lose their jobs, the situation can quickly reach a crisis point, as has been clearly shown in the 'credit crunch' and recession experienced by many countries in recent years.

Part 3: Exam practice

Task 1: Model answer

The line graph shows economic growth over a 15-year period ending in 2010. The pie charts give a breakdown of household spending in four separate years over the same period. Viewed together, there appears to be a relationship between economic growth and patterns of spending.

According to the graph, economic growth began at a modest 1 per cent, rose modestly, then remained more or less steady at about 2 per cent until 2003. It grew sharply and peaked at nearly 5 per cent in 2005, then fell dramatically to -5 per cent in 2008, before recovering to 1 per cent in 2010.

Over the same period, changes in patterns of spending were evident. In periods of low or negative growth, spending on housing and food accounted for a larger proportion of total household expenditure than in times of relative prosperity. Conversely, in times of economic growth, spending on less essential items such as travel, entertainment and clothing tended to increase. This is particularly evident in the chart for 2005 where together these three items appear to account for over 15 per cent of total spending.

In summary, the figures show that in times of hardship, households spend a greater proportion of their income on necessities whereas, in times of prosperity, more is spent on non-essentials.

Task 2: Model answer

Learning to manage money is something that virtually everyone must do as the ability to maintain a balance between income and expenditure is essential for a stable life. In many developed countries, the availability of easy credit and a wide variety of financial products have made the task of managing one's money more complex. In less affluent parts of the world, lack of money or access to credit creates its own challenges. In this essay, I will outline two ways in which people can learn to manage their money.

Learning by example is one important method. From their early years, children can observe how their parents make financial decisions. They may notice, for example, whether money is saved for costly purchases, or whether purchases are bought on credit. Children can also see what kinds of criteria parents use when choosing what to buy, for instance, whether quality or quantity is more important. It is important, therefore, that parents model sensible purchasing behaviour and explain what they are doing and why. However, in many circumstances, this may not be sufficient.

Another important means of teaching people to manage money is through education. When school children, for instance, learn arithmetic, they could also be taught the basics of budgeting and how to recognise good value. For adults, the Internet could be a good source of advice on how to save money. Price comparison websites, for example, can be a good way of researching what is available before making an expensive purchase.

The ability to manage money is often taken for granted. Because the consequences of poor money management can be severe, it is worthwhile taking steps to ensure people are as well-informed as possible.

8   Children and parents

Part 1:   Vocabulary

Exercise 1
a iv 4,   b iii 3,   c v 1,   d i 5,   e ii 2,
The nouns on the left can be used to refer to people; the nouns on the right refer to life stages.

Exercise 2
Rights: a, d, f, g, h
Responsibilities: b, c, e, i, j

Exercise 3
1 forced
2 empowered
3 compelled
4 have a duty to do
5 coerced into joining

Exercise 4
1 over
2 in
3 with; on
4 with
5 of
6 of; into
7 from; for
8 in; of

Exercise 5
1 in the best interests of
2 taken into account
3 cooperate with others
4 interfering too much in their lives
5 exercise too much control over.

Part 2:   Practice exercises: Task 1

Exercise 1
1 Response 2 is more satisfactory because it includes examples from the table to support the main point.
2 The writer wants to emphasise the difference in opinion between parents and adolescents, so he/she has chosen those details that illustrate the biggest gap in views.
3 superlatives (*most control, the biggest conflict*) and the preposition *with* (*with nearly 80% of mothers believing*)
4 Yes (*roughly three out of four parents*). N.B. It is not always necessary to signpost supporting examples because an experienced academic reader will expect main points to be followed by examples.

Exercise 2
Overall, parents said that they wanted significantly more control over their children than did the adolescents surveyed. The areas where parents wanted <u>most control</u> were how adolescents spend their free time and what friends they make. Roughly three out of four parents wanted to place restrictions on these areas, whereas only approximately one in five children felt this was needed. <u>The biggest conflict</u> of opinion concerned young people's choice of friends <u>with</u> nearly 80 per cent of mothers believing they should exercise control and only 17 per cent of adolescent girls agreeing.

1 Women predominated in schools for children. This was <u>particularly</u> true of schools for very young children. Over 95 per cent of nursery school teachers, <u>for example</u>, were female. The situation was similarly one-sided in primary schools, <u>where</u> over 90 per cent of teachers were women.
2 In Arts and Social Science-related subjects, UK students tended to do better. <u>The biggest gap</u> in performance was in International Law, <u>where</u> three-quarters of UK students gained a second class degree or better. In contrast, fewer than half of the international students attained this level.
3 There are four types of writing system in which characters represent sounds. <u>The oldest of these</u> is 'Abjad', <u>in which</u> each character represents a consonant sound. Arabic, <u>for instance</u>, uses this type of system.

Exercise 3
1 only (or sole),   2 where,   3 particularly (or most),   4 biggest (or widest),   5 only

Exercise 4
Suggested answer
The adolescent boys surveyed also indicated a greater acceptance of parental control than did the adolescent girls. The two areas where girls accepted greater control were how they spend their free time and how they spend their money. The biggest gap between boys and girls was over what subject they study. 45 per cent of boys said they agreed with parental restrictions in this area, where as only a third of girls felt this was needed.

Part 2:   Practice exercises: Task 2

Exercise 5
a 4, b 7, c 1, d 3, e 2, f 5, g 8, h 9, i 6

1 present simple tense
2 five
3 *can* because this task 2 question asks you to make suggestions

4 *should* is a less emphatic term than *must* and is used to express necessity; *may* is used to express a possibility and to 'hedge'

Exercise 6
1 would
2 may/might
3 should/must
4 can/could
5 can/could

6 would
7 might/may/could
8 can/could
9 would
10 could/would

Exercise 7
1 In short
2 In brief, In summary, In conclusion
3 a
4 d

5 Society can ensure that children's rights are taken into account, that children have access to help, and that children are properly informed of their rights.

Exercise 8
Suggested answer
In summary, there are several ways in which young people can be encouraged to behave responsibly. They can be involved in defining what constitutes good behaviour, and they can be taught leadership skills. Parents and teachers should be encouraged to try these methods before resorting to more punitive measures. If they are successful, they may very well discover a maturity in their children that they never anticipated.

Part 3:   Exam practice

9 An ageing population

Part 1: Vocabulary

Exercise 1
1 b, 2 b, 3 a, 4 b, 5 a, 6 b, 7 a

Exercise 2
1 f, 2 e, 3 i, 4 a, 5 h, 6 j, 7 b, 8 c, 9 g, 10 d

Exercise 3
Causes: b, c, f, h   Consequences: a, d, e, g

Exercise 4
1 e, 2 g, 3 h, 4 c, 5 d, 6 a, 7 f

Part 2: Practice exercises: Task 1

Exercise 1
Decreasing birth rates can be attributed to two main factors, namely, availability of family planning <u>and</u> changes in how people feel about work and family. These changes include greater career aspirations among women, a tendency to delay marriage, <u>and</u> a preference for smaller families. Lower mortality, on the other hand, is due to increased longevity, <u>which</u> results from improved health care <u>and</u> better living conditions.

Exercise 2
The graph illustrates two trends, namely: the rise in the proportion of the world's population aged sixty-five and above and the decline in the proportion of those under five. As can be seen, the proportion of elderly people has risen gradually from approximately 5 per cent in 1950 to roughly 7.5 per cent today. Over the next thirty years, it is expected to more than double. The proportion of young children, on the other hand, has fallen gradually since 1970 from approximately 14 per cent to 9 per cent. It is forecast to continue falling at roughly the same rate over the next forty years.

Exercise 3
1 The bar chart shows the percentage of people in seven different countries who were over the age of sixty-five in 2000 and the percentage of people expected to be in that age group in 2030.
2 Korea, Mexico, and Turkey, all developing or newly industrialized countries, are expected to experience large increases in the proportion of the population that is elderly.
3 The biggest increase is likely to occur in Korea, where the proportion of pensioners is expected to increase from 10 per cent to 35 per cent.
4 The changes in all three countries will occur from a relatively low base, so the predicted proportion of elderly residents will still be lower than that expected in developed economies.

Exercise 4
Suggested answer
The figure shows the distribution of the population in terms of gender and age. The age group with the highest percentage of both men and women is 55 to 59. Roughly five per cent of the population is in this age group. The age groups with the next highest proportion of the population are 30 to 34 and 35 to 39. Interestingly, until the age of fifty-nine, the proportion of males and females is roughly equal. However, thereafter, women make up a higher proportion of the elderly population. This trend is particularly evident in those aged eighty plus. Over four per cent of women fall into in this category, whereas only two per cent of men have reached this age.

Part 2: Practice exercises: Task 2

Exercise 5

1 *A number of measures can be taken to ensure that the elderly can enjoy life after retirement.*
2 *measure*
3 *measure* occurs in the first (topic) sentence of each of the following two body paragraphs
4 *older people, the elderly, elderly people, all, increasingly frail section of the population*
5 *sums of money, savings*

Exercise 6

1 Synonyms for *younger family members* could include: *the younger generation, younger relatives, younger relations, younger members of the family*
   Synonyms for *older relations* could include: *the older generation, older family members, older relations, elderly relatives, senior members of the family*
2 Circle *arguments*; mandatory retirement age
3 Circle *consequences*; population ageing

Exercise 7

1 development/shift
2 concerns/disadvantages/drawbacks
3 strategy/measure/approach
4 process

Exercise 8

1 The most fundamental obligation that younger family members have towards older relations is to ensure that their physical needs are being met.
2 Another core obligation is to ensure that older relations continue to feel a sense of love and belonging.
3 Finally, younger family members should ensure that older relations continue to have the opportunity to grow and develop as individuals.

1 One of the main consequences of population ageing is the increasing incidence of illnesses and ailments commonly associated with age.
2 Another consequence is growing pressure on care givers, often sons and daughters who may themselves be in the process of raising a family of their own.
3 The final consequence is pressure on pension funds.

Paragraph
Suggested answer

One of the main consequences of population ageing is the increasing incidence of illnesses and ailments commonly associated with age. Cancer, heart disease, and arthritis, for example, are all on the rise in many countries with ageing populations. This trend can result in pressure on health budgets and services.

Part 3: Exam practice

Task 1: Model answer

The line graph shows three demographic trends in Scotland between 1940 and 2020: birth rate, population growth rate, and death rate.

The birth rate followed a falling trend overall from 2.5 per cent in 1940 to a projected 0.5 rise in 2020. There were brief increases in the late 1940s and 1960s followed by more substantial falls, particularly between 1950 and 1960.

The population growth rate followed a very similar trend with a brief time lag, suggesting a strong link between birth rate and population rate. The main difference in the two trends was a more substantial rise in population growth between 1945 and 1955.

The death rate showed a somewhat different trend. There was a steady fall between 1940 and 1955, followed by a very gradual decline over the next forty-five years. There is expected to be a slight rise over the next decade, presumably as the 'boom' generation of 65–75 years previously reaches the end of its life span.

Overall, the trends show a declining population in Scotland.

Task 2: Model answer

People today can expect to live a longer and healthier life than people in the past. People often see retirement as a time for relaxation and letting go of the stresses of working life. However, many who reach retirement age are more interested than ever in contributing actively to their communities. This essay will outline two ways in which this interest can benefit society.

Becoming involved in schools is one of the ways in which the life experience of the elderly can be made available to the community. Because families now are often more mobile than in the past, many children do not have regular contact with grandparents. Yet children are often fascinated by stories of life in the past. Inviting local retired people into schools to speak to children can help to maintain a vital link between past and present.

Another way in which society can benefit from a more active older generation is by inviting older employees to remain in work part-time. Older people may not want to or indeed be able to do a full day's work; however, their experience may continue to be valuable to their employers. A good example of this can be seen in one scheme in the UK in which elder employees remained in work as mentors for younger employees.

Schools and the workplace are just two of the areas in which those who have reached retirement age can continue to contribute to their communities. As life expectancy improves, the need to maintain an active and socially meaningful life may also increase. Experience suggests that this trend can have benefits for all, not just the elderly.

10 Fame

Part 1: Vocabulary

Exercise 1
1 e, 2 f, 3 c, 4 h, 5 b, 6 a, 7 d, 8 i, 9 g

Exercise 2
1 impression
2 aspirations
3 image
4 fame
5 flawed
6 icon

Exercise 3
1 well-known/famous/legendary
2 imperfect/bad/worthless
3 like/admire/idolise
4 recognition/praise/acclaim

Exercise 4
1 Inevitably ...
2 Unfortunately ...
3 Fortunately ...
4 Surprisingly ...
5 Obviously ...
6 Interestingly ...
7 Importantly ...

Exercise 5
1 Less obviously ...
2 More importantly ...
3 Not surprisingly ...
4 Somewhat surprisingly ...

Part 2: Practice exercises: Task 1

Exercise 1
1 past
2 percentage
3 except
4 rose
5 than
6 smaller
7 in contrast
8 feature
9 rose
10 smaller
11 past
12 feature
13 except

Exercise 2
1 significant
2 Many
3 For example
4 Surprisingly
5 did not
6 appear

Exercise 3
1 featured
2 occupations
3 those surveyed
4 opting for
5 career
6 occupied

Exercise 4
Suggested answers
1 One of the most significant advances in civilization is the development of modern methods of food production and preparation.
2 Convenience foods have now become the norm in many societies.
3 Although some people idealise traditional cooking practices and believe they will prevail indefinitely, ...
4 In more traditional societies, where families tended to be large, it made economic sense for one person to devote him/herself to time-consuming domestic tasks such as growing and preparing food.
5 Nowadays, people tend to live in ever smaller family units.
6 If each family were to spend large amounts of time growing and processing food, this would be a poor use of society's human resource.
7 ... the increase in the number of adults, especially women with children, who work in full-time employment.

Exercise 5
1 receiving, 2 percentage, 3 negative, 4 small,
5 On the other hand, 6 was not, 7 there appears to be
Underline: those surveyed, people questioned, those who took part in the survey, survey respondents

Part 2: Practice exercises: Task 2

Exercise 6
Suggested answers

1 benefit, positive consequence
2 drawback, negative consequence
3 view, point of view
4 nevertheless
5 individuals
6 dilemma, difficulty
7 approach, strategy
8 significant, noteworthy
9 topic, concern
10 circumstances, context

Exercise 7
1 Paragraph c is the best.
2 Paragraph a is too informal; paragraph b has too few hedges; paragraph d has too much repetition.

Exercise 8
Suggested answer

In the past, people (1) *generally* became famous for ***their achievements***. Einstein, Dickens, and Gandhi, for instance, were all celebrated for ***their contributions to*** science, literature and public life. People were interested in them (2) *primarily* because they were role models.

One of the reasons fame today is so different is because celebrities (3) *appear to* meet a range of people's emotional needs, not just the need for role models. ***Many*** celebrities today are famous simply for being famous. The public are (4) *often* interested in them because, when news of scandals ***emerges***, they (5) *can experience* the satisfaction of feeling superior to people they have been encouraged to envy.

Exercise 9
Suggested answer

Another reason fame today is unique is the desire for ordinary people to explore the nature of fame itself. Many celebrities that have emerged from reality television programmes, for example, come from the same walks of life as ***the viewing public***. Reading about or watching ***such people*** allow ***ordinary individuals*** to imagine what it might be like to suddenly find themselves in the public eye. ***People who are famous for being famous*** may, therefore, allow ***unremarkable people*** to indulge in wish-fulfilment fantasies without having to worry about whether they are capable of significant achievement.

The third, and perhaps most significant reason that celebrities play such an important role in modern life is the fact that commercial pressures encourage media organisations to focus on information that is immediately attractive to ***the consumer***. As we have seen, the '***cult of celebrity***' appears to tap into powerful emotional needs, the need to feel superior, the need to imagine oneself to be the centre of attention; therefore, ***celebrity news*** sells.

Exercise 10
Suggested answer

In brief, the nature of fame today is ***somewhat*** different from fame in the past. There ***appears*** to be a greater need to denigrate, rather than celebrate the actions of people in the public eye, as well as a ***consuming*** interest in fame itself. Whether the public will eventually ***grow*** tired of ***these remains to be seen***.

Part 3: Exam practice

Task 1: Model answer

The table gives the results of an opinion poll in which respondents were asked about their views of celebrity news coverage.

There were clear majority views for all three questions asked. The vast majority of those questioned (85%), for example, said that there was too much news coverage of celebrities. Only 7 per cent said there was the right amount, and an even smaller percentage (6%) said there was too little.

The public was somewhat more divided on the question of who was responsible for the quantity of celebrity news. A majority (56%) said the news organisations were; however over a third felt that the public were at fault. Roughly one in ten respondents felt that both were responsible.

When asked to identify the news medium responsible for providing most of the coverage, most of those polled singled out television news programmes. Online news websites were identified by 15 per cent of respondents, followed by newspapers (12%).

Overall, the findings suggest that most people think there is too much focus on celebrities in the news and that television news programmes are largely to blame.

Task 2: Model answer

In the past, news about famous people may have been confined to gossip columns in newspapers; these days it is not uncommon for celebrities to feature as front page news. There is evidence that the public feels there is too much news coverage of famous people. Not surprisingly, there is concern about how this might be affecting people, and in particular children.

One of the possible negative consequences of the 'cult of celebrity' is the tendency to confuse fame and notoriety. Celebrity scandals are just as likely to receive publicity as celebrity achievements. Indeed, some famous people have received more attention for their misuse of drugs and alcohol than for their successes on the stage or in sports. Children who crave attention may come to see misbehaviour as normal.

The emphasis on individuals in the public eye may also be at the expense of serious news coverage. Next to the superficial excitement of celebrity gossip, news about serious events and issues that have a more profound effect on people's lives may seem uninteresting. Children may be forming a very distorted picture of how the world works.

The negative influence of celebrities on children can also be seen in children's career aspirations. These days, young people are much more likely to see themselves as potential sports stars or entertainers. The prevalence of these figures in the mass media may convey the impression that such positions are plentiful. Children may be developing unrealistic expectations that they too will become rich and famous.

In summary, the 'cult of celebrity' may be affecting children in a number of undesirable ways. It is important that children be taught to critically evaluate what they see in the media so that they can form a more realistic view of society, acceptable behaviour, and indeed themselves.

11 The car

Part 1: Vocabulary

Exercise 1
a 2, b 7, c 8, d 1, e 4, f 6, g 5, h 3

Exercise 2
1 cycle routes
2 speed cameras
3 pedestrians; danger
4 traffic queues
5 motorways
6 road works
7 bus lanes

Exercise 3

verb	noun
reduce	reduction
produce	production
convert	*conversion*
maintain	*maintenance*
emit	emission
combust	*combustion*
propel	*propulsion*

Exercise 4
1 propelled
2 converting
3 propulsion
4 reduce
5 combustion
6 emissions
7 emit
8 maintenance
9 produce
10 production

Exercise 5
a achievement, b appearance, c allowance, d explanation, e involvement, f provision, g opposition

1 opposition, 2 achievement, 3 explanation, 4 appearance, 5 provision, 6 allowances, 7 involvement

Part 2: Practice exercises: Task 1

Exercise 1
1 a, 2 b, 3 b, 4 a, 5 c, 6 b

Exercise 2
1 decreased
2 are expected
3 correlates
4 varied
5 accounted
6 were asked

Exercise 3
1 driving
2 to use
3 purchasing
4 change
5 travelling
6 to reduce

Exercise 4
1 the, 2 by, 3 -, 4 on, 5 to, 6 -, 7 with; of,
8 the, 9 -, 10 to, 11 a, 12 a, 13 the, 14 the

Part 2: Practice exercises: Task 2

Exercise 5
a 9, b 2, c 1, d 5, e 4, f 7, g 6, h 3, i 8, j 10

1 The **evidence shows** that wearing a seatbelt significantly reduces road accident fatalities. (countable vs. uncountable noun)
2 In fact wearing a seatbelt is **the** most important safety measure that can be taken. (use of the article)
3 The number of road accidents **declined** last year. (tense)
4 It is **illegal** to drive without a licence. (word class)
5 The cost of insurance depends **on** several factors including age, experience and type of car. (preposition)
6 Organisations such as the AA **can provide** assistance to motorists who break down. (verb form)
7 Many people **who** live in rural areas have no choice but to travel by car. (relative clause)
8 Buying a second-hand car is sometimes **risky. Inexperienced** buyers can be easily cheated. (run-on sentence)
9 There **are** numerous examples of illegal practices in the second-hand motor trade. (subject-verb agreement)
10 **This is because** the industry is poorly regulated and buyers are not always well-informed. (sentence fragment)

Exercise 6

1 Cars undoubtedly have practical benefits for the people who own them.
2 Urban pollution, which is largely caused by vehicle emissions, can lead to respiratory problems such as asthma.
3 Noise pollution (which is) caused by cars is another problem that can affect people's health.
4 The vast majority of car journeys are for short distances, which can be covered on foot.
5 There is evidence that people who live on streets with high volumes of traffic are less likely to know or interact with their neighbours.

Exercise 7

1 Although most people say they would use other forms of transport for short journeys, in fact, most car journeys are for distances of less than two miles.
2 Most people are reluctant to buy an electric car because of three factors: cost, maintenance and reliability.
3 Some of those surveyed said they had concerns about the distance electric cars could travel before having to be recharged.
4 Electric cars are more expensive than conventional cars. However, their maintenance costs are lower.
5 One major Japanese car manufacturer, which produces some of the most fuel-efficient petrol-powered cars, has recently announced that it plans to invest more heavily in electric car technology.
6 By 2025, over 40 per cent of vehicles on the road are likely to be hybrid or electric cars.
7 Hybrid and electric cars produce fewer emissions, but this may not result in a reduction in overall emissions because the growth in car ownership over the next fifteen years is likely to accelerate.

Exercise 8

1 As people in many parts of the world now have greater access to cars, they often have more choice over where they live and work.
2 Cities have become more sprawling because people have sought out the greater privacy and space afforded by suburban living.
3 There are more vehicles, often travelling at greater speed; as a consequence, the streets are less hospitable to pedestrians.
4 There has also been a decline in public transport; as a result, people have less day-to-day contact with other members of their community.
5 Since most people are very dependent on their cars, they do not want to give them up.

Exercise 9
Suggested answer

In many parts of the world, people now have greater access to cars. ***Therefore***, they often have more choice over where they live and work. Cities have become more sprawling, ***as*** people have sought out the greater privacy and space afforded by suburban living. ***Because*** there are more vehicles, often travelling at greater speed, the streets are less hospitable to pedestrians. There has also been a decline in public transport. ***As a consequence,*** people have less day-to-day contact with other members of their community.

Exercise 10
Suggested answer

One of the ***factors*** that distinguishes developed from developing economies is mass car ownership. Cars undoubtedly have practical benefits for the individuals ***who*** own them. They allow for more flexible and autonomous travel. Like other consumer items, they can be used ***to express*** individual taste and identity. ***However***, they also clearly have a number of undesirable consequences.

One of these consequences is ***deterioration*** in people's health. Urban pollution, which is largely ***caused*** by vehicle ***emissions, can*** cause respiratory problems such as asthma. ***These*** health problems ***are*** more prevalent in cities, particularly among children and the elderly. Noise pollution caused by ***cars*** is another problem that can ***affect*** people's health.

Another ***consequence*** of car use is a decline in levels of physical activity and hence levels of fitness. Although this is partly a consequence of rising prosperity generally, there is evidence that car use is responsible ***for*** lower levels of cardiovascular fitness. The vast majority of car journeys are for less than two miles, that is, distances that can easily be covered on foot. In short, when people own **cars**, they tend to walk less, thus removing a major means by which people maintain day-to-day fitness.

Finally, widespread car use can have a negative effect on community life. There is **evidence** that people who live on streets with high volumes of traffic are less likely to know or interact with their neighbours. This too can have a negative impact on people's sense of well-being.

These factors alone are unlikely to discourage people from buying cars. However, more could be done to make the public more aware of the disadvantages of car ownership. **Providing** alternative means of transport would encourage people to use their cars less and enjoy some of the benefits of a car-free environment.

Part 3: Exam practice

Task 1: Model answer

The table compares modes of transport used in four countries: the USA, the UK, France and the Netherlands. Percentages of journeys made by car, bicycle, public transport and on foot are given. The bar chart shows the results of a survey into reasons people in the USA travel to work by car.

As can be seen from the table, cars were the most frequently used form of transport in all four countries. However, the proportion of journeys made by car ranged from a low of 47 per cent in the Netherlands to a high of 90 per cent in the USA. Figures for the other forms of transport also varied considerably. Not surprisingly, in the Netherlands, a high proportion of trips were made by bicycle (26%) and on foot (18%). The highest rate of public transport use was in France, where nearly one in five journeys was made by public transport.

The bar chart provides information that may help explain why car use is so high in the USA. The most frequently cited reason was lack of any other alternative (38%). Although a sizable percentage said it was more convenient (21%), the other factors listed appeared to relate more to need than preference, e.g. working night shift.

Overall, the figures show considerable variation in modes of transport used, though the car continues to dominate in most contexts.

Task 2: Model answer

Mass car ownership clearly has a number of undesirable consequences for people's health and fitness as well as for the environment and community life generally. Nevertheless, owning a car is still seen as a desirable option. In fact, the number of cars in the world today is fast approaching one billion. Although this trend may seem inexorable, there is much that can be done to discourage unnecessary car use.

One possible approach is to make cars expensive to own and use, for example, by taxing them at the point of purchase or annually through a road tax. Certain types of car use, for instance short journeys within already congested cities, can also be discouraged through road pricing schemes such as that operating in London. However, these punitive measures alone are unlikely to have a major impact unless alternative means of transport are available.

Evidence suggests that where public transport options are plentiful, convenient and reliable, people will use them. Inhabitants of cities such as Paris, which have invested heavily in commuter rail networks, are more likely to use public transport than people living in cities where such networks have been allowed to deteriorate.

A less expensive and more environmentally sound option is to create a network of cycle lanes and other facilities for cyclists, such as safe weather-proof shelters for parking bicycles. This has the additional advantage of encouraging people to keep fit whilst allowing them the flexibility of autonomous travel. Cities in the Netherlands, which have relatively high rates of cycling, have shown how this can work.

In brief, the trend towards rising car ownership and use need not be inexorable. People can be encouraged to use other means of transport. However, rhetoric alone is unlikely to bring about change. Investment in practical alternatives is what is needed above all.

12   Practice test

Task 1: Model answer

The bar chart shows information about people's smoking behaviour by age group in the UK. Several trends are evident.

The highest proportion of those who have never smoked (nearly two-thirds) was in the 16 to 24 year group. The proportion tended to decrease with age. Only 40 per cent of people aged 65 to 74 had never smoked.

On the other hand, the percentage of those who had quit smoking tended to increase with age. Only 5 per cent of those in the youngest age group (16 to 24) were ex-smokers, as opposed to roughly 40 per cent of those aged 65 to 75.

The percentage of those classed as heavy smokers also showed a distinct pattern. People in middle age (35 to 54) tended to be the heaviest smokers - approximately 13 per cent of the total. A relatively small proportion of those in the youngest age group, and an even smaller percentage of those in the oldest group (roughly 3 per cent) smoked heavily.

Overall, age appears to be a significant factor in patterns of smoking behaviour.

Task 2: Model answer

The issue of equality and achievement has occupied people throughout history. Some argue that because people vary in terms of talent and initiative, inequality is inevitable. The job of the government is to ensure freedom for each person to achieve his or her personal best. Others believe that because wealth and therefore opportunity tend to concentrate in the hands of a few, the government must actively redistribute resources. While I believe there is some truth in both views, the latter is likely to yield greater life satisfaction for the majority.

Societies that are very unequal in terms of income and resources are often credited with great achievements. The United States, for example, has many successful individuals in business and science. Its universities, among the world's most expensive, rank among the top ten in the world and employ a disproportionately large number of Nobel-prize winners. However, such countries also often produce many people without qualifications, and poor prospects.

More egalitarian countries often achieve higher average rates of success. Finland and Korea, for example, which invest heavily in free public education for all, tend to rank high in international comparisons of literacy and numeracy rates. Although such countries do not always produce many internationally successful 'superstars', they tend to have a high proportion of moderately successful people in terms of employment and income. More importantly, they have lower rates of absolute deprivation and underachievement.

In short, if we allow freedom for individuals to achieve their potential, some inequality is inevitable. However, success usually generates wealth, which can be passed from one generation to another resulting in inequality of opportunity regardless of individual merit. It, therefore, makes sense for society to level the playing field.